From Roots to Radiance: Women's Health through Every Stage

OrangeBooks Publication

1st Floor, Rajhans Arcade, Mall Road, Kohka, Bhilai, Chhattisgarh 490020

Website: **www.orangebooks.in**

First Edition, 2025

ISBN: 978-93-7426-976-3

Price: Rs. 300.00

Printed in India

From ROOTS to RADIANCE

Women's Health Through Every Stage

NITYA BYRRAJU

OrangeBooks Publication
www.orangebooks.in

Table of Contents

Chapter - 1
Introduction: Why Your Health Matters to Everyone You Love

Chapter - 2
Growing Up - From Girl to Young Woman

Chapter - 3

Marriage and Pregnancy - A New Phase of Life

Chapter - 4

The Next Phase - Perimenopause, Menopause, and Beyond

Chapter - 5

Staying Strong in Later Years

Chapter - 1

Introduction: Why Your Health Matters to Everyone You Love

When you take care of your health, amazing things happen. You don't just feel better - you help your whole family feel better too. Your health affects your children, your partner, your friends, and your community.

But here's the problem: many women think taking care of themselves is selfish. They think they should take care of everyone else first. This way of thinking hurts everyone - including the people they're trying to help.

Your health is not a luxury. It's not something only rich women can have. Your health is your strength. And when you are strong, everyone around you becomes stronger too.

Pic 1: https://www.vecteezy.com/

Why Your Health Matters to Your Family

You Are the Heart of Your Home

Think about your daily life. You probably do a lot for your family. You cook meals, take care of sick children, remember doctor appointments, and worry about everyone's problems. You are like the center of a wheel-everything revolves around you.

When you feel good, everything works better. When you're tired, stressed, or sick, everything becomes harder for everyone.

Let's say you learn how to handle stress better. Maybe you learn to take deep breaths when you feel worried. This doesn't just help you - it helps your whole family. Your children see you staying calm. They learn to stay calm too. Your partner feels less stressed because you're less stressed.

Or think about exercise. When you walk or move your body regularly, you have more energy. You can play with your children more. You can do things with your family. You show them that being active is important.

Pic 2: https://www.shutterstock.com/

Money and Security

Your health affects your family's money too. When you're healthy, you can work. You can earn money for your family. You don't have to spend lots of money on doctor visits and medicines.

It's much cheaper to stay healthy than to get sick and then try to get better. Regular check-ups cost less than emergency room visits. Eating good food costs less than treating diabetes. Exercise is free, but heart surgery is very expensive.

When women in a community are healthy, the whole community does better. Healthy women can work, start businesses, and help their neighborhoods grow.

Pic 3: https://www.istockphoto.com/

Being a Leader in Your Community

Women often hold families and communities together. You check on elderly neighbors. You help friends with their problems. You organize events at your children's school.

When you're healthy - both in your body and mind - you can do these things better. You have energy to help others. You can think clearly about problems. You can be the person others turn to for help.

If you've learned to deal with sadness or worry, you can help other women who feel the same way. Your story of getting healthier can inspire others to take care of themselves too.

Pic 4: https://www.vecteezy.com/

How Your Health Affects Your Children's Future

Before and During Pregnancy

Your health affects your children even before they're born. If you eat well and feel good before getting pregnant, your baby has a better start in life.

During pregnancy, everything you do affects your baby. Good food helps your baby's brain grow. Managing stress helps prevent problems. Women who are healthy before and during pregnancy usually have healthier babies.

These healthy babies often grow up to be healthier children and adults. They do better in school. They have fewer health problems. They learn to make good choices about their own health.

Teaching by Example

Children learn more from watching you than from listening to your words. If they see you eating vegetables, they'll want to eat vegetables too. If they see you exercising, they'll think exercise is normal and important.

When you take time to walk, you're teaching your children that being active matters. When you choose healthy food, you're showing them how to take care of their bodies. When you manage stress in healthy ways, you're teaching them skills they'll use their whole lives.

Pic 6: https://www.freepik.com/

Breaking Bad Patterns

Sometimes families pass down bad health habits from parents to children. Maybe your mother never exercised, so you never learned to exercise. Maybe your family always ate unhealthy food, so that's what you know how to cook.

When you decide to be healthier, you can break these patterns. You can be the first person in your family to eat well, exercise regularly, or take care of mental health. Your children will grow up knowing these healthy habits are normal.

This is especially important for diseases that run in families, like diabetes or heart problems. Even if these diseases are in your family, you can often prevent them or make them less serious by staying healthy.

Pic 7: https://www.womensrunning.com/

Creating a Good Home

Healthy mothers create better homes for their children. When you feel good, you have more patience. You can handle problems better. You can give your children the love and attention they need.

When you're not stressed all the time, you're less likely to yell at your children. You can listen to their problems. You can help them when they need it. You create a safe, loving place where children can grow up strong and confident.

Pic 8: https://www.vecteezy.com/

Your Health Is Your Strength

What Real Strength Means

Many women think being strong means never taking care of themselves. They think they should always put others first, even if it makes them sick or tired.

This is wrong. Real strength means taking care of yourself so you can take care of others. Think of it like this: if you don't eat, you can't cook for your family. If you don't sleep, you can't take care of sick children. If you don't take care of your mental health, you can't help others with their problems.

Taking care of yourself isn't selfish - it's smart. It's the best way to take care of everyone you love.

You Can Afford to Be Healthy

You might think you can't afford to be healthy. You might think healthy food costs too much, or gym memberships are too expensive. But many of the most important things for your health don't cost money.

Walking is free. Drinking water instead of soda saves money.

Getting enough sleep doesn't cost anything. Taking deep breaths when you're stressed costs nothing. Spending time with friends and family is free and good for your mental health.

Yes, some parts of healthcare cost money, and this can be hard. But even small steps toward better health can make a big difference in how you feel and how much energy you have.

Pic 9: https://www.vecteezy.com/

Small Changes Make Big Differences

You don't have to change everything at once. Small changes can grow into big improvements over time.

Maybe you start by walking for 10 minutes every day. After a few weeks, you might find you sleep better. When you sleep better, you have more energy. When you have more energy, you might start eating better. When you eat better, you feel even stronger.

Each good choice makes the next good choice easier. Success builds on success.

Pic 10: https://www.istockphoto.com/

Health Gives You Power

When you're healthy, you feel more in control of your life. You have energy to work toward your goals. You can think clearly about decisions. You feel confident about trying new things.

This confidence doesn't just help with health - it helps with everything. Women who take charge of their health often find they can take charge of other parts of their lives too. They might go back to school, start a business, or speak up for what they believe in.

Your Journey Starts Today

Getting healthy doesn't mean you have to be perfect. You don't have to completely change your life overnight. You just need to start somewhere.

As you read this book, remember that taking care of yourself is one of the best things you can do for your family and community. When you're healthy and strong, you can help others be healthy and strong too.

Every woman deserves to feel good. Every woman deserves to have energy. Every woman deserves to be healthy. This includes you.

Your health matters. Your strength helps others. And you can start building that strength with your very next choice.

You have the power to be healthy. You have the right to take care of yourself. And you have people who need you to be strong.

Your health is your strength. Use it.

Pic 11: https://www.shutterstock.com/

Chapter - 2
Growing Up - From Girl to Young Woman

Priya's First Period

Priya was only twelve when it happened. She was in her math class, copying sums from the blackboard, when she felt something strange between her legs. It was wet and uncomfortable. At first, she thought she had spilled water. But when she went to the bathroom, her heart almost stopped— there was blood on her underwear.

Her hands shook. "Did I hurt myself? Am I sick?" she whispered. She tried wiping with tissue

paper, but the blood didn't stop. Fear rose inside her. She didn't want anyone to know. Too embarrassed to tell her teacher, she sat quietly for the rest of the day, using layers of toilet paper to manage.

When she got home, she quickly changed her clothes, hiding the stained underwear under her bed. That night, she could hardly sleep. She kept thinking, *What if something is really wrong with me?*

Pic 12: https://www.instagram.com/reel/Cz8f-jVyR4z/

The next morning, when the bleeding continued, Priya finally gathered courage and told her mother. Her mother's face softened with love and understanding. She hugged Priya and said gently, "My dear child, don't be scared. You got your period. You are not sick. You are becoming a young woman."

At that moment, Priya felt a wave of relief. She wasn't dying, she wasn't broken—she was simply growing.

Learning about Her Body

That evening, Priya's mother sat with her. She explained that a girl's body is designed by nature to one day carry a baby. Even though Priya was still very young and not ready to be a mother, her body had already started preparing itself. This monthly bleeding was part of that preparation.

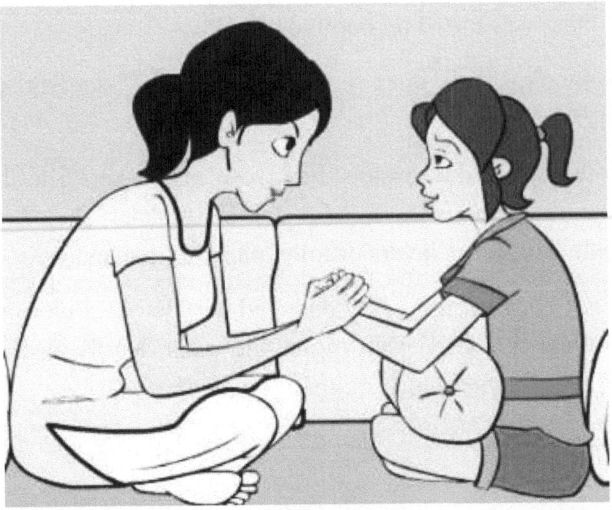

Pic 13: https://www.linkedin.com/pulse/generation- gap-power-acceptance-bhavya-mangla

To help Priya understand better, her mother drew a small diagram on a piece of paper. "See," she said, "this is your uterus. Think of it like a small room inside your belly, about the size of your fist. This is where a baby grows when a woman becomes pregnant. On each side of the uterus are two small organs called ovaries. They are like little storage boxes that hold thousands of tiny eggs. Each month, one egg comes out and travels through a small passage called the fallopian tube. If the egg does not meet a man's seed, it simply dissolves. The uterus then cleans itself, removing the soft lining it prepared. That cleaning comes out as blood. This is your period."

Priya listened carefully. She realized that her body was not punishing her—it was following a natural rhythm that every girl experiences.

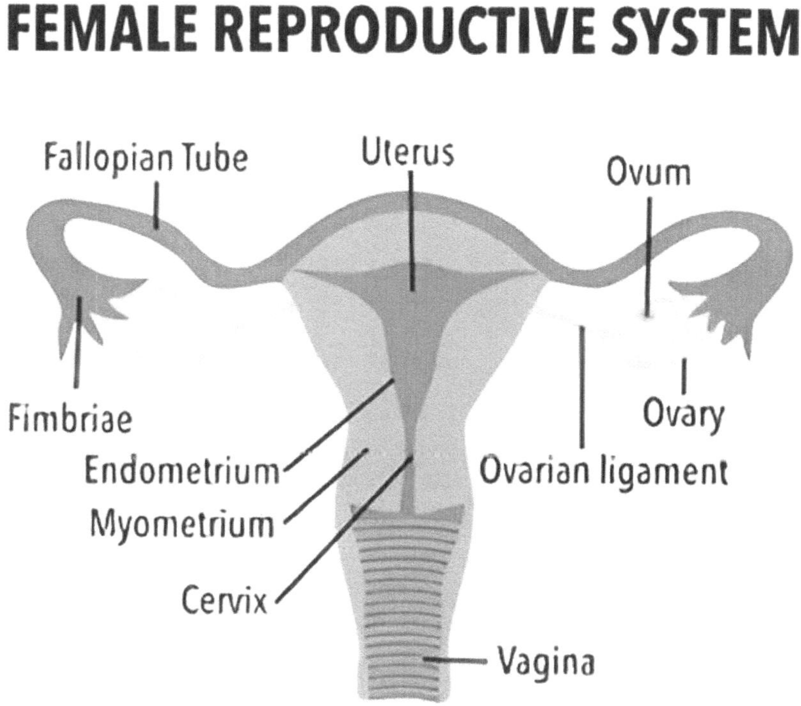

Pic 14: https://www.shutterstock.com/

Understanding the Menstrual Cycle

Her mother explained more. "The cycle usually takes around 28 days, though it can be a little shorter or longer—sometimes 21 days, sometimes up to 35. It is like a clock inside your body, repeating every month."

1. **First Stage – Preparing the Room:** The uterus builds a soft lining, like preparing a comfortable bed for a baby.
2. **Second Stage – The Egg's Journey:** One ovary releases an egg, and it travels through the fallopian tube.
3. **Third Stage – Waiting Time:** The body waits to see if the egg will meet a seed and form a baby.
4. **Fourth Stage – Cleaning:** If no baby is formed, the uterus cleans itself, and that cleaning flows out as blood—this is the period.

Her mother smiled and said, "This is not dirt or waste. This is your body's way of staying healthy."

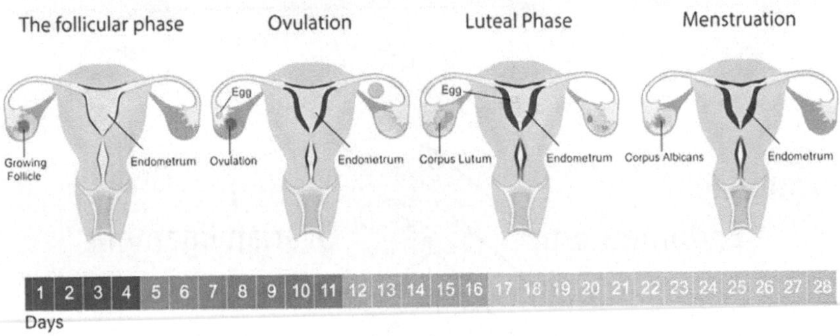

Pic 15: https://www.shutterstock.com/

Myths vs. Scientific Facts

Priya looked nervous. She whispered, "But my friends said that when a girl gets her period, she is dirty and should not go into the kitchen or temple."

Her mother shook her head. "That is only a myth. Science tells us the truth. A girl on her period is not dirty. She is perfectly clean. She can cook, pray, touch food, and go anywhere. Some people in society have created wrong beliefs, but we should not be ashamed of our bodies."

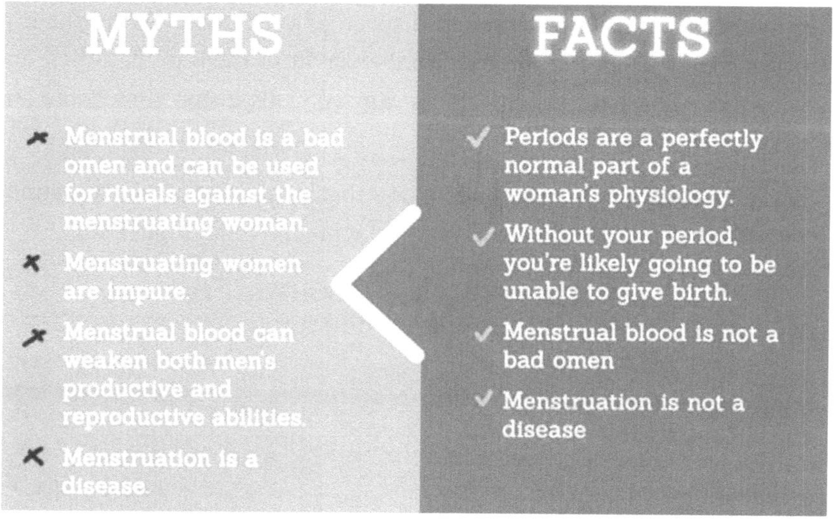

Pic 16: mariestopes.org.gh – facebook page

She added, "Another myth is that girls should not bathe during their period. But bathing is very important. A warm bath actually makes you feel fresh and can reduce pain. Exercise is also safe. Simple walking or stretching can help reduce cramps."

Priya felt comforted. She realized she did not have to hide or feel ashamed of her periods.

Staying Clean and Safe During Periods

Her mother then showed her how to take care of herself. She gave Priya a packet of sanitary pads and explained how to use them. "You should wear this inside your underwear to absorb the blood. Change it every three to four hours, even if it is not fully soaked, to stay fresh and prevent infection."

She also explained that washing the private area with plain water twice a day is enough. Soap should only be used outside, never inside, because harsh soaps can cause irritation. Priya was told to wear clean cotton underwear every day and always wash her hands before and after changing pads.

Her mother also explained how to dispose of used pads. "Wrap them in paper and throw them in the dustbin. Never flush them in the toilet, and never leave them open where others can see. This keeps your home and environment clean."

Priya felt stronger now. She understood that periods were not something to be scared of but something to manage with knowledge and care.

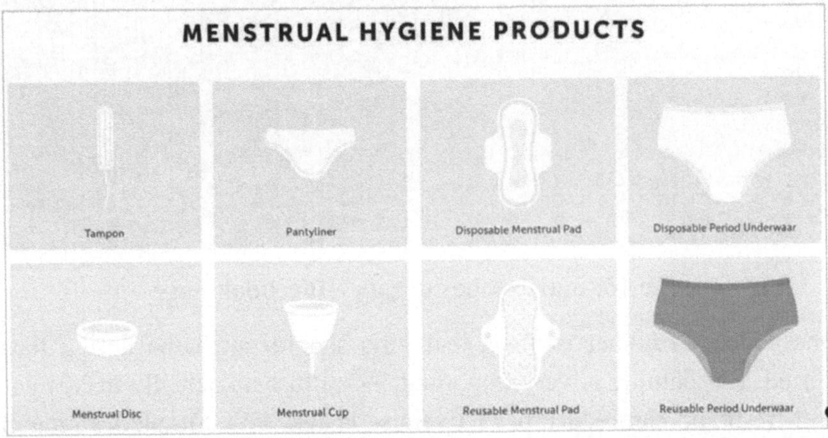

Pic 17: https://www.shutterstock.com/

The Changes of Puberty

As Priya settled into understanding her periods, she noticed other changes happening in her body. One morning while brushing her hair, she caught her reflection in the mirror and realized her chest looked different. Her breasts had started to grow. At first, they were small, tender bumps that sometimes felt sore. Priya was embarrassed and wore loose clothes to hide them.

Her mother reassured her, "This is normal, beta. Every girl goes through it. Breasts grow slowly over a few years and may feel tender at times. Eventually, they will look different from your friends' or cousins' because no two women's bodies are the same. That is perfectly okay."

She also explained that hair would start growing in new places—underarms, legs, and around the private area. Priya noticed this too and felt awkward. Her mother explained, "This hair is a sign of growing up. Some girls remove it, some don't. That is your choice. But always keep clean, especially underarms and private areas, to avoid bad smell and infections."

Priya also noticed her skin becoming oily, and sometimes pimples appeared on her face. Her mother comforted her, "Acne is common in teenagers. Wash your face with plain water, avoid touching pimples too much, and eat healthy food. Don't worry—it usually gets better with age."

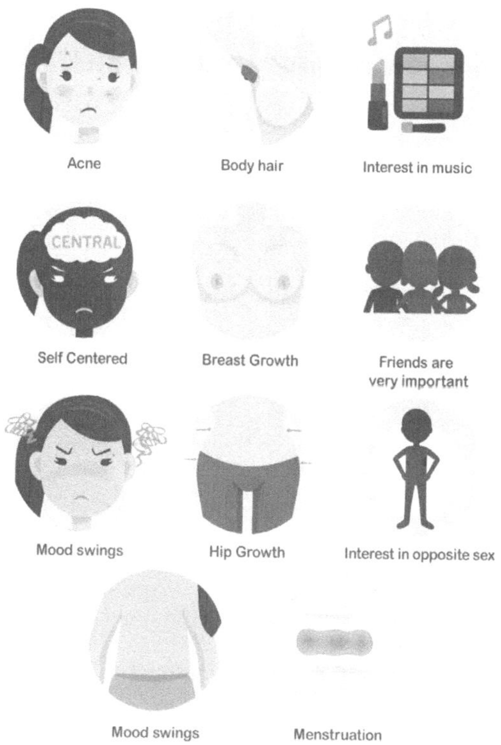

Pic 18: https://www.shutterstock.com/

Understanding Emotions during Puberty

Puberty wasn't only about physical changes. Priya sometimes felt moody—angry at her brother for no reason, or suddenly sad while watching a movie. At other times, she laughed loudly and felt excited without knowing why.

Her mother gently explained, "This happens because of hormones. Hormones are like little messengers in your body. During puberty, they increase and change, which makes you feel strong emotions. Sometimes you may cry, feel angry, or feel like no one understands you. That's normal."

She added, "The best way to manage these feelings is to talk. Don't keep everything inside. Share with me, a friend, or even write in a diary. Physical activity also helps—go for a walk, play a game, or dance to music. It keeps the mind lighter."

Priya realized she wasn't "strange" or "over-sensitive." She was simply growing, and these feelings were a natural part of it.

Pic 19: https://www.vectorstock.com/

Knowing Your Body – A Simple Anatomy Lesson

One evening, Priya's mother decided to give her a clear understanding of her body parts. She drew another diagram, labeling the important organs of the female reproductive system:

- **Uterus** – the small, hollow organ where a baby can grow.
- **Ovaries** – two tiny oval-shaped organs that release eggs.

- **Fallopian Tubes** – the narrow passageways that carry the egg from the ovary to the uterus.
- **Vagina** – the passage that connects the uterus to the outside of the body. This is where menstrual blood flows out, and later in life, where a baby is delivered.
- **Cervix** – the narrow opening between the uterus and the vagina.

Her mother explained slowly and clearly: "Knowing your body is power. Many girls grow up not even knowing what is inside them, and then they believe wrong stories. But when you understand, you can take care of yourself better."

Priya felt proud that she now knew the scientific truth.

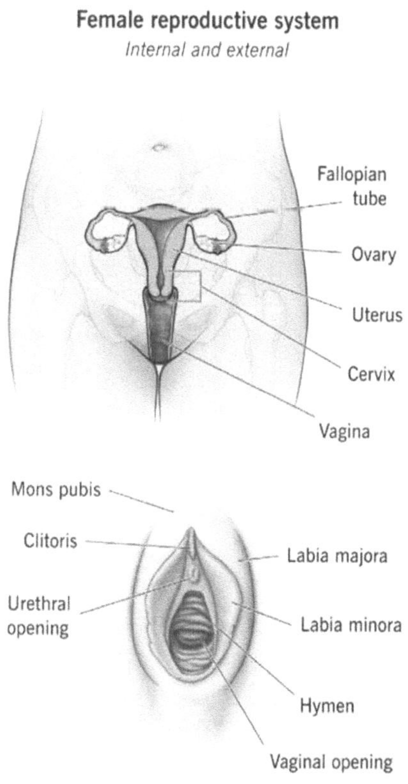

Pic 20: https://my.clevelandclinic.org/health/articles

Nutrition for a Healthy Teenager

As Priya's periods became regular, her mother noticed she often felt tired, especially during the bleeding days. She explained, "When you lose blood, your body also loses iron. That can make you weak or dizzy. So you must eat food that gives you strength."

Her mother made sure Priya had iron-rich foods like spinach, jaggery, lentils, and eggs. She encouraged Priya to eat seasonal fruits, plenty of vegetables, and drink enough water.

She also said, "Don't skip meals. Breakfast is important, especially now. And avoid too much junk food like chips and sugary drinks. Sometimes they make you feel tired instead of energetic."

Priya realized that food was not just about taste—it was like medicine that kept her body strong and her periods healthier.

Pic 21: https://www.vecteezy.com/

Common Problems during Periods

One month, Priya had very painful cramps. She lay curled up in bed, holding her stomach, with tears in her eyes. "Why does it hurt so much?" she asked.

Her mother explained, "Many girls get cramps during their periods. It happens because the uterus squeezes itself to push out the blood. You can try a hot water bag on your stomach, gentle exercise, or even simple breathing. Avoid lying in bed all day— moving a little actually helps."

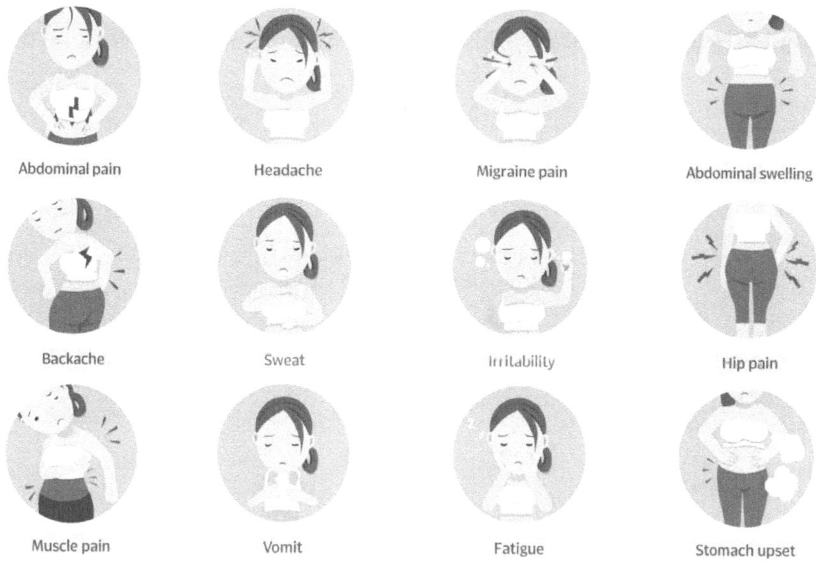

Pic 22: https://www.dreamstime.com/stock-illustration- menstrual-pain-treatment-info-graphic-vector- illustration-image64753750

She also explained that if cramps were very severe, or if Priya ever had very heavy bleeding (changing pads every hour), or missed periods for many months, she should see a doctor. "Sometimes our body gives signals that it needs extra care. It's important to listen to those signals."

Priya nodded. She understood that some discomfort was normal, but extreme problems needed medical attention.

Hygiene and Self-Care

As Priya grew more comfortable with her periods, her mother reminded her that keeping herself clean was just as important as managing the bleeding. She explained, "During your period, always change your pad or cloth regularly. If you keep it for too long, germs can grow and cause itching or infection."

Her mother showed her how to wash the private area gently with clean water, not with harsh soaps that could cause irritation. "Your body has its own way of staying clean inside," she said. "So don't use powders or strong perfumes near your private area. They can harm more than help."

Pic 23: https://www.facebook.com/meesa.np

Priya also learned that underwear should be washed daily and dried in sunlight whenever possible, since sunlight kills germs.

If privacy was a concern, her mother suggested drying clothes indoors but making sure they were completely dry before use.

"Cleanliness is part of dignity," her mother reminded her. "When you care for your body, you also respect yourself."

Privacy, Confidence, and Self-Esteem

One day, Priya overheard her classmates whispering about her because she had a small stain on her skirt. She felt deeply embarrassed and didn't want to return to school the next day. That evening, she tearfully told her mother, "I feel ashamed. Everyone must think I'm dirty."

Her mother hugged her tightly. "Never feel ashamed, beta.

Periods are natural. Without them, no human life would exist. If someone teases you, it only shows their ignorance, not your weakness."

She advised Priya to always carry an extra cloth or pad in her school bag, along with a small scarf to tie around her waist if needed. "These small precautions give you confidence," she said.

Priya slowly realized that confidence wasn't about hiding her womanhood—it was about carrying herself with pride. She reminded herself, "If my body can do this every month, it must be strong."

Pic 24: https://www.shutterstock.com/

Peer Pressure and Body Image

As months passed, Priya noticed that some of her friends were taller, while others had fuller breasts or clearer skin. She sometimes compared herself and felt she wasn't pretty enough.

Her mother gently explained, "Every flower blooms in its own time. Some girls grow faster, others slower. But each has her own beauty. Never compare your body with someone else's. It's like comparing a rose with a lotus—both are beautiful in their own way."

She also warned Priya about peer pressure. "Sometimes friends may tell you to try skin creams, or to act older than you are, or even to start relationships you are not ready for.

Remember, your value is not in looking like someone else, but in knowing who you are."

Priya understood that true beauty came from self-respect, health, and confidence—not from copying others.

Pic 25: https://www.shutterstock.com/

Preparing Emotionally for Teenage Years

Priya's mother knew that the teenage years bring many challenges—not just in the body, but also in the mind. She explained, "As you grow, you will have new friendships, new attractions, and sometimes new conflicts. These are all part of life. What matters is how you handle them."

She advised Priya to build good habits: studying regularly, exercising, eating well, and resting enough. She also reminded her that saying "no" was sometimes necessary. "If something feels wrong—whether it's a suggestion from a friend or pressure from anyone—trust your inner voice. That voice is your guide."

Priya asked, "What if people think I'm rude for saying no?"

Her mother smiled. "Then let them. Protecting your dignity is more important than pleasing everyone. A strong woman is one who respects herself first."

This gave Priya courage. She realized that growing up wasn't only about getting periods or developing breasts—it was also about becoming emotionally strong and wise.

Pic 26: https://www.vecteezy.com/

Looking Ahead

By the end of her first year of puberty, Priya felt more confident. She understood her body better, knew how to care for herself, and was learning to manage her emotions. Most importantly, she felt supported by her mother's words and knowledge.

Her journey was just beginning, but she knew she was not alone. Many girls in her community would also go through the same changes, and Priya dreamed of sharing what she had learned so they too would feel less afraid and more prepared.

Chapter - 3
Marriage and Pregnancy - A New Phase of Life

Priya Gets Married

Priya was now 22 years old. She had finished her studies and found a job at a local school. Her family arranged her marriage to Raj, a kind young man who worked at a bank. Both families were happy with the match.

Before her wedding, Priya's mother and aunt sat down with her for an important conversation. "Marriage brings new responsibilities and changes to your body," her mother said gently. "We want to make sure you're prepared and healthy."

Pic 27: https://in.pinterest.com/

Preparing for Marriage - Reproductive Health

Understanding Sexual Health

"When you get married, you and your husband will want to be close to each other physically," Priya's aunt explained. "This is called sexual intercourse or making love. It's a normal and healthy part of marriage."

Sexual intercourse is when the husband's penis enters the wife's vagina. This is how babies are made when the time is right. It should never hurt when done properly and with care. Both husband and wife should want to participate.

It's normal to feel nervous the first time. Take things slowly and communicate with your husband. If it hurts, stop and try again later with more patience. It's okay to ask questions and learn together.

Pic 28: https://www.dreamstime.com/

Family Planning

"You don't have to have babies right away," Priya's mother explained. "It's good to wait until you're both ready - emotionally and financially."

There are many reasons to wait before having children. You need time to get to know your husband better and save money for baby expenses. It's important to make sure you're both healthy and enjoy being married for a while before adding the responsibilities of parenthood.

There are several methods to prevent pregnancy. Condoms are the safest option for new couples. Birth control pills require a doctor's prescription and must be taken daily. Injectable contraceptives are shots given every three months. An IUD is a device that a doctor places inside your uterus. Natural family planning involves tracking your fertile days during your menstrual cycle. Always discuss family planning with your husband and a doctor. Both partners should agree on when to have children, and a healthcare provider can help you choose the best method for your situation.

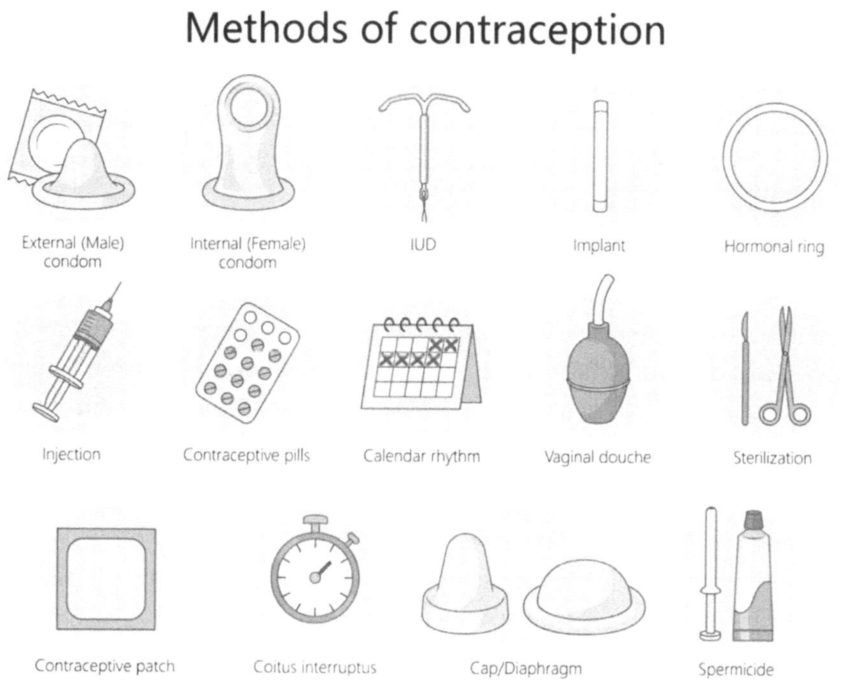

Pic 29: https://stock.adobe.com/

Pre-Marriage Health Check

Before her wedding, Priya visited a doctor for a health check- up. The doctor recommended several tests including a blood test for anemia, blood pressure check, weight and height measurement, and a general health examination. She also needed tests for infections and vaccination updates like tetanus.

Important infection tests before marriage include blood tests for HIV/AIDS, which checks for the virus that causes AIDS, and Hepatitis B, which checks for liver infection that can be passed to others. A syphilis test checks for a bacterial infection that can be treated, and a complete blood count checks for any blood infections.

Urine tests are also important. A urinary tract infection test checks for bladder or kidney infections, and a general urine examination checks for any infections in the urinary system.

Other important tests include tuberculosis screening, which checks for lung infection that spreads through air, thyroid testing to ensure the gland is working properly, and blood sugar testing to check for diabetes. For women who have been sexually active, a Pap smear checks for cervical infections and abnormal cells, and STD screening checks for sexually transmitted infections.

These tests are important to protect your health by finding and treating infections early. They also protect your partner since some infections can spread between spouses, and protect future babies since some infections can harm unborn children. Having these tests gives peace of mind knowing you're both healthy before starting married life. Most infections can be treated easily if found early.

Don't be worried about these tests. They are routine and normal procedures. Having a test doesn't mean doctors think you have an infection. Most results come back normal, and if any infection is found, most can be treated easily. It's always better to know and treat than to ignore potential problems.

These tests matter because they ensure you're healthy for marriage, help detect any problems early, ensure you're ready for pregnancy when you want it, and protect both you and your future husband.

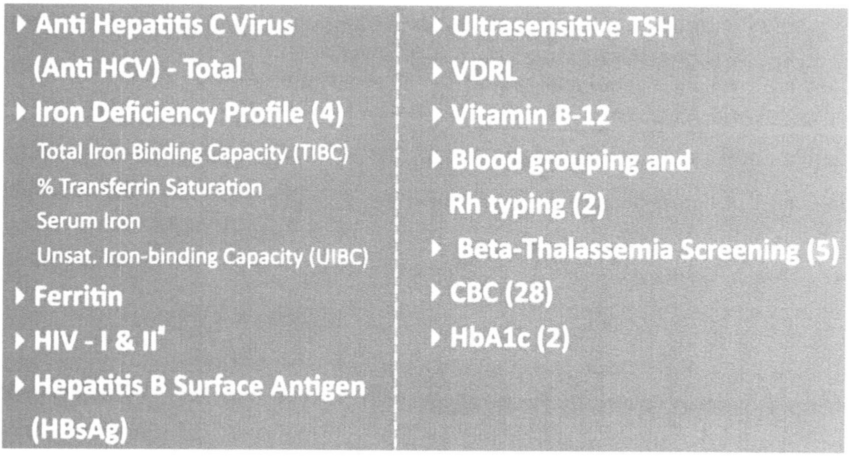

Pic 30: https://millenniumpathologylab.com/

Special Care for Women Living in Underserved communities (Slums)

Living in underserved community areas creates extra health challenges. Here's what you need to know to stay safe:

Hygiene Challenges and Solutions

Common problems include shared toilets that may not be clean, limited water supply, overcrowded living conditions, poor drainage with standing water, and problems with insects and rats.

Pic 31: https://www.dreamstime.com/

To stay clean despite these challenges, you should boil water if you're not sure it's clean, then let it cool before drinking.

Wash your hands frequently, especially before eating, after using the toilet, and after touching anything dirty. Keep your personal items separate and don't share towels, soap, or undergarments with others. When using shared toilets, clean the seat before use if possible, or squat without touching the surface. Dispose of menstrual pads properly by wrapping them in paper and putting them in the designated area.

If you can't boil water, you can make it safer by letting it sit in sunlight for six or more hours in clear plastic bottles. You can also add one drop of bleach per liter of water if it's available. Always cover stored water to keep it clean and prevent contamination.

Infections More Common in Underserved community Areas

Waterborne diseases are particularly common in underserved community areas. Diarrhoea and dysentery cause loose, watery stools that sometimes contain blood. Typhoid presents with high fever, headache, and stomach pain. Hepatitis A causes yellow eyes and skin, dark urine, and stomach pain.

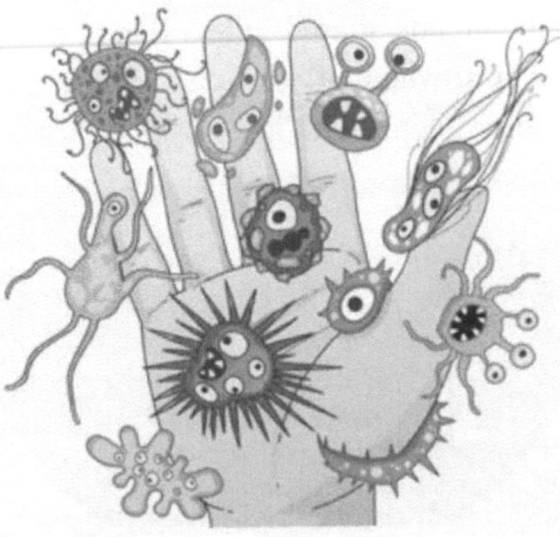

Pic 32: https://www.shutterstock.com/

Air-borne diseases spread easily in crowded conditions. Tuberculosis causes a persistent cough for more than two weeks, along with weight loss and night sweats. Respiratory infections cause cough, fever, and difficulty breathing.

Skin and eye infections are also common. Scabies causes intense itching, especially at night, with small bumps appearing on the skin. Fungal infections create itchy, red patches on the skin. Eye infections make eyes red, watery, and painful.

Vector-borne diseases spread through mosquitoes and flies. Malaria causes high fever, chills, sweating, and severe headaches. Dengue presents with high fever, severe headache, pain behind the eyes, and body aches. Chikungunya causes fever, severe joint pain, and rash.

To prevent these diseases, use mosquito nets while sleeping and remove any standing water around your home. Keep food covered at all times and maintain distance from people who are coughing. Most importantly, seek medical help early if you develop any persistent symptoms.

Pregnancy Challenges in Underserved community Areas

Living in underserved communitys creates extra risks during pregnancy. There's a higher chance of infections due to poor sanitation, and malnutrition is common due to limited access to nutritious food. Anemia is very common due to poor diet and repeated infections. It can be difficult to reach hospitals during emergencies, and there may be a lack of clean birthing facilities.

Pic 33: https://www.shutterstock.com/

There are critical symptoms that require immediate medical attention. Severe bleeding during pregnancy, where you're soaking more than one cloth per hour, is extremely dangerous. A severe headache with blurred vision could indicate dangerous high blood pressure. Continuous vomiting, where you're unable to keep any food or water down for 24 hours, requires immediate care. High fever over 101°F with chills, severe abdominal pain that doesn't get better, and baby not moving for more than six hours after 28 weeks of pregnancy are all emergencies. Water breaking before 37 weeks and fits or convulsions also require immediate hospital care.

When healthcare is far away, it's crucial to know your nearest health center and how to get there quickly. Save money specifically for emergency transport and identify someone who can help you get to the hospital quickly. Learn to recognize danger signs so you know when you must seek help immediately.

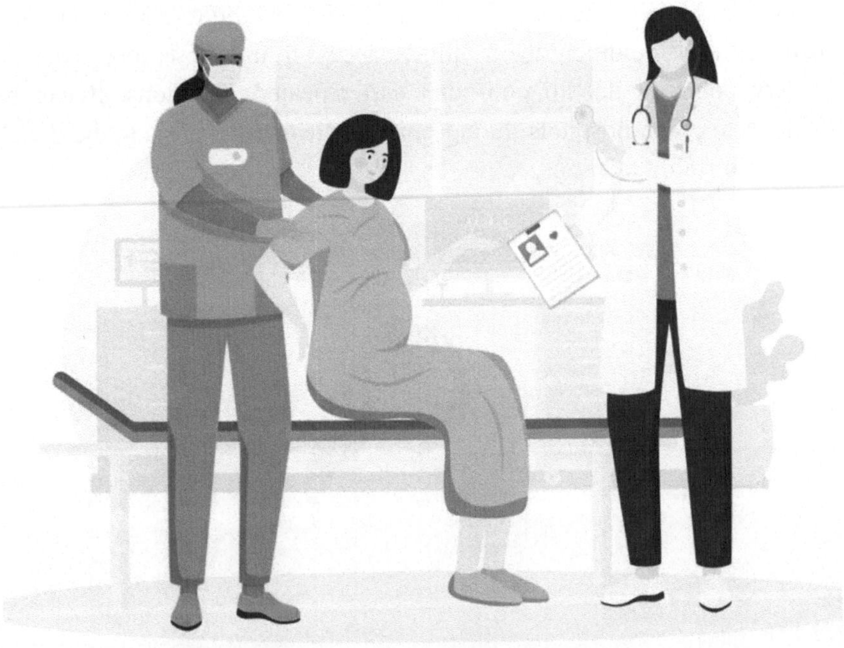

Pic 34: https://www.shutterstock.com/

Nutrition Challenges in Underserved community's

Common nutritional problems in underserved community areas include iron deficiency anemia, which is very common and causes weakness and pregnancy complications. Protein deficiency affects the baby's growth, while vitamin deficiencies can cause birth defects. Not getting enough calories leads to babies with low birth weight.

Despite limited resources, there are affordable nutritious foods available. Green leafy vegetables like spinach and fenugreek leaves are high in iron. Pulses and beans provide protein and iron at relatively low cost. Eggs provide complete protein and are affordable. Seasonal fruits contain vitamin C, which helps with iron absorption. Jaggery contains iron and is cheaper than other sweets. Groundnuts provide protein and healthy fats.

Watch for danger signs of malnutrition, including extreme fatigue and weakness, very pale skin, nails, or inner eyelids, swelling in feet and hands, hair falling out or becoming very thin, not gaining weight during pregnancy, and babies measuring small during check-ups.

Pic 35: https://www.shutterstock.com/

To make the most of limited food resources, eat small amounts frequently rather than a few large meals. Combine foods strategically by eating vitamin C foods like tomatoes and lemons with iron-rich foods like spinach and beans. Don't skip meals even if food is limited. Avoid empty calories by limiting tea, sweets, and fried foods. If available, cook in iron pots, which can add iron to your food.

Safe Delivery in Underserved community Conditions

Planning for delivery is crucial when living in underserved community conditions. Identify a skilled birth attendant in your area and know the location of the nearest hospital that provides delivery services. Save money specifically for delivery expenses and emergency transport. Prepare clean cloths and basic supplies ahead of time. Arrange help from experienced women in your community.

If you must deliver at home, clean the area as much as possible and boil water, letting it cool for washing. Anyone helping should wash their hands thoroughly. Use clean clothes that have been boiled if possible. Cut the umbilical cord with a clean blade that has been boiled first. Get to a health center as soon as possible after delivery.

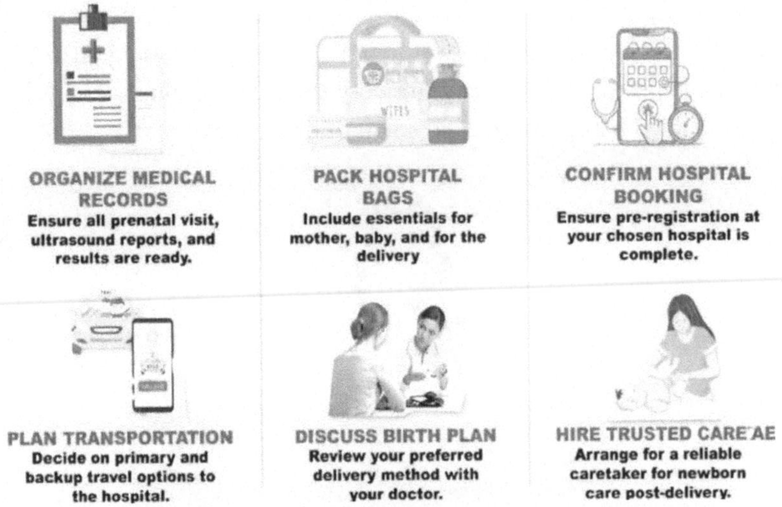

Pic 36: https://drmadhugoel.com/

Watch for danger signs during labor. Labor lasting more than 18 hours for a first baby, heavy bleeding that's more than normal period flow, the baby's cord coming out before the baby, the mother having fits, the baby not breathing after birth, and retained placenta that doesn't come out within one hour all require immediate medical attention.

Post-Delivery Care in Underserved communities

Preventing infections after delivery requires keeping the delivery area clean for at least six weeks. Wash your hands before touching your breasts or baby. Boil water for washing if regular water is dirty. Change clothes frequently, especially if they get soiled. If possible, isolate yourself from sick family members.

Breastfeeding presents unique challenges in underserved community conditions. Limited privacy in crowded conditions, poor nutrition affecting milk production, pressure from others to give water or other foods too early, and the need to work soon after delivery all create difficulties.

Pic 37: https://pixabay.com/

Solutions include exclusive breastfeeding for six months with no water or other foods needed. Eat extra food to support milk production. Find a quiet corner or use cloth for privacy while nursing. Feed frequently to maintain your milk supply.

After delivery, watch for warning signs including heavy bleeding after the first week, severe abdominal pain, high fever with chills, bad-smelling discharge, severe headache that doesn't go away, red, hot, painful areas on your breast, and signs of depression such as no interest in your baby or feeling hopeless.

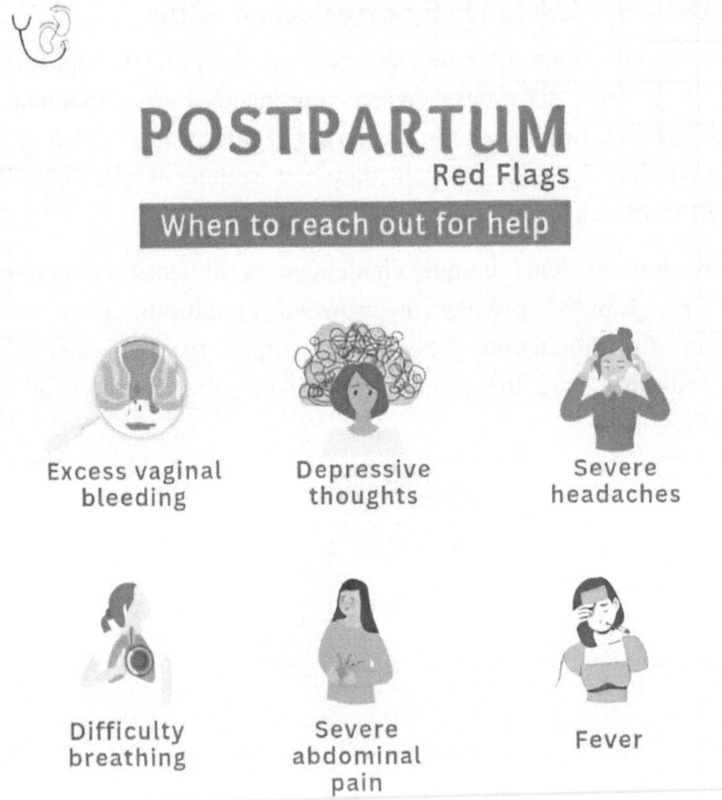

Pic 38: https://www.instagram.com/p/DFCYOniTdOR/

Family Planning in Resource-Limited Settings

Affordable contraception options are available even in resource-limited settings. Condoms are available at government health centers. Birth control pills are provided free at government clinics. IUD insertion is available free at government hospitals. Injectable contraceptives are available at low cost.

Natural family planning methods include the calendar method, where you track your menstrual cycles. Breastfeeding delays fertility but is not 100% reliable. The withdrawal method is not very reliable but is better than no protection at all.

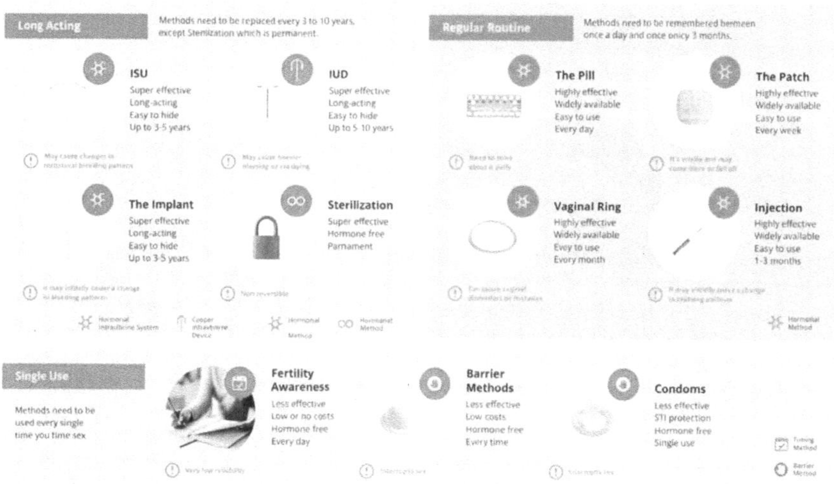

Pic 39: https://venngage.com/

You can get help from government health centers, NGO clinics in your area, community health workers, and ASHA (Accredited Social Health Activist) workers.

Building Support Networks

It's important to know key people in your community. The ASHA worker in your area can provide basic health advice.

Experienced older women who have had healthy pregnancies can share valuable knowledge. Find the local midwife, but ensure they use clean practices. Know your nearest government health worker.

Community resources include self-help groups for women that can provide emotional and financial support.

Government schemes offer maternal and child health programs.

NGO programs often provide free health education and services. Religious or community centers may offer health camps.

Pic 40: https://www.yumpu.com/

When to Definitely Seek Medical Help

Never try to handle these situations at home: heavy bleeding during pregnancy or after delivery, high blood pressure symptoms like headache, blurred vision, and swelling, signs of infection such as fever and bad-smelling discharge, baby not moving normally, severe abdominal pain, difficulty breathing, and severe depression or thoughts of hurting yourself or your baby.

Remember that free government healthcare is available for pregnant women. Don't let money stop you from seeking emergency care. It's better to go to the hospital unnecessarily than to miss a serious problem. Your life and your baby's life are more important than any other consideration.

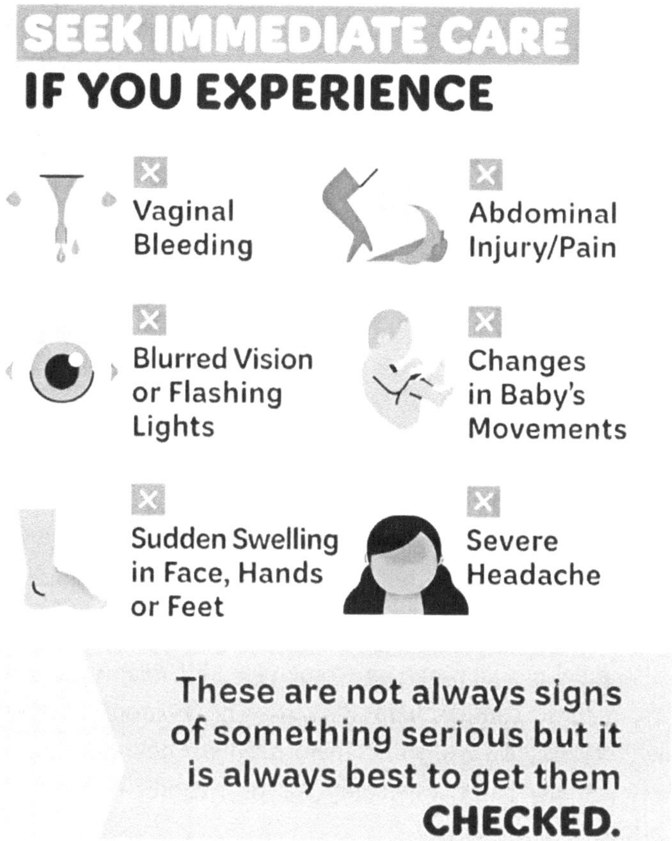

Pic 41: https://www.facebook.com/

Emergency Preparedness for Underserved community Dwellers

Prepare an emergency kit that includes clean clothes that have been boiled and dried, soap for hand washing, a clean blade that's been boiled in case of home delivery, phone numbers of the nearest hospital and health center, a small amount of money saved for emergency transport, and important documents like ID cards and any medical papers.

Create a transportation plan by knowing what transport is available, such as auto, taxi, or ambulance services. Identify neighbors who can help in emergencies and know the fastest route to the nearest hospital. Have a backup plan if your main transport isn't available.

Develop a communication plan by teaching family members to recognize danger signs, knowing important phone numbers by heart in case you can't access written ones, and identifying someone who can make calls if you're unable to.

Common Harmful Myths in Underserved community Communities

There are dangerous beliefs that you should avoid. Some people believe that pregnant women should eat less to have smaller babies for easier delivery, but the truth is that eating less causes malnutrition and increases complications. Proper nutrition is essential for both mother and baby.

Another myth is that dark green vegetables cause dark skin in babies, but the truth is that green vegetables provide essential nutrients and don't affect the baby's skin color. Some people think that taking iron tablets makes the baby's skin dark, but iron prevents dangerous anemia and is essential for healthy pregnancy.

There's also a belief that pregnant women shouldn't eat eggs or meat, but protein from these sources helps the baby grow properly. Some think home delivery is always safer than hospital delivery, but hospital delivery is actually safer, especially for first babies or when there are complications.

People sometimes believe that giving water to newborns prevents dehydration, but breast milk provides all the fluid needs, and water can cause dangerous infections. Another myth is that heavy bleeding after delivery is normal for several weeks, but heavy bleeding is actually dangerous and needs immediate medical attention.

Finally, some believe that traditional healers can treat all pregnancy problems, but some problems need modern medical treatment to save the mother's and baby's lives.

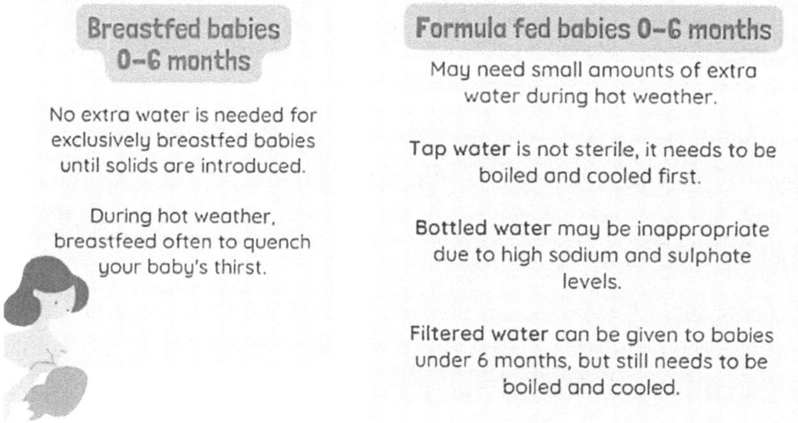

Pic 42: https://www.facebook.com/photo.php?fbid=5234131006693775&id=800298956743691&set=a.907207809386138

Recognizing Medical Emergencies

During pregnancy, life-threatening situations that require immediate hospital care include bleeding with clots or soaking more than one pad per hour, severe headache with spots in vision or swelling of face and hands, persistent vomiting where you can't keep food or water down for 24 or more hours, high fever over 101°F especially with chills, severe stomach pain that doesn't improve with rest, no baby movement for six or more hours after 28 weeks of pregnancy, a gush of water before 37 weeks indicating early labor, and convulsions or fits.

During labor, emergency signs include labor longer than 18- 20 hours without progress, heavy bleeding that's more than a normal period, the cord coming out before the baby, the baby's arm or leg coming first instead of the head, and the mother becoming unconscious or having fits.

After delivery, watch for heavy bleeding where you're soaking more than one pad per hour, large blood clots bigger than your palm, severe abdominal pain that gets worse, high fever over 100.4°F with chills, bad-smelling discharge from the vagina, breast becoming hard, red, and hot with fever, severe headache with vision problems, and thoughts of hurting yourself or your baby.

Making Healthcare Accessible

Free government services are available to help you. Janani Suraksha Yojana provides money for institutional delivery.

Free medicines are available at government hospitals. Free tests during pregnancy are provided at government centers. Free immunizations are available for both mother and baby. Emergency transport through the 108 ambulance service is also available.

To access these services, visit the nearest PHC (Primary Health Center) or government hospital. Carry any ID proof such as voter ID, Aadhaar card, or ration card. Don't pay money if services are supposed to be free. If you're denied free services, complain to higher authorities. Use your ASHA worker to help navigate the system.

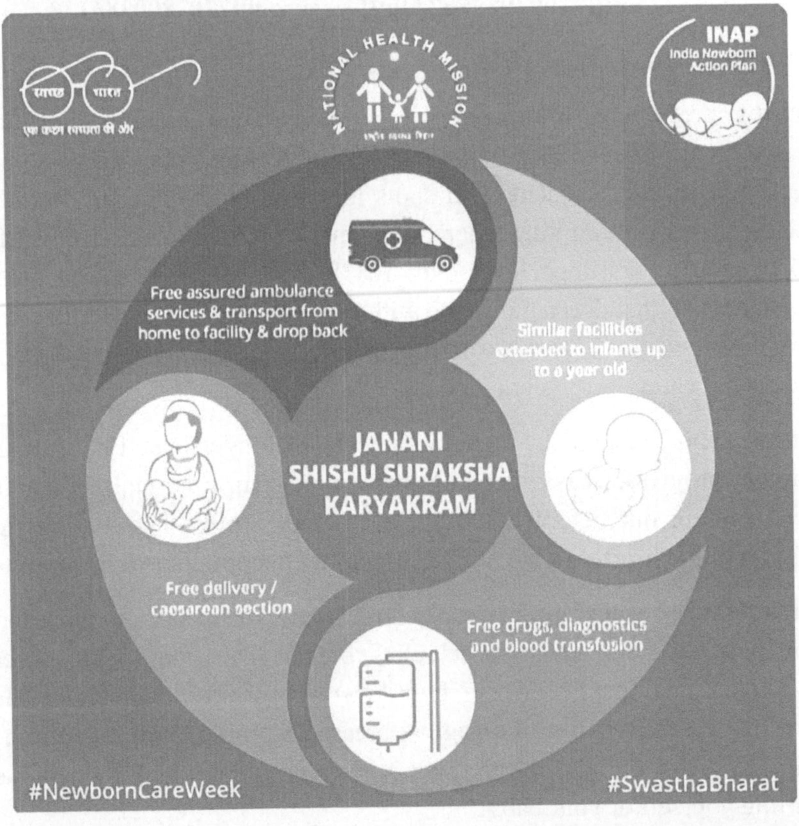

Pic 43: https://x.com/MoHFW_INDIA/status/9321339239283 71200

You have important rights that you should know about. You have the right to emergency treatment even without money upfront. You have the right to respectful treatment regardless of your economic status. You have the right to information about your health condition and the right to a second opinion if you're not satisfied with treatment. You also have the right to complain about poor quality care.

Building Health Awareness in Your Community

Share the knowledge you gain by teaching other women what you learn about health. Form groups to discuss women's health issues. Invite health workers to speak to your community and challenge harmful myths when you hear them.

Take community actions to improve conditions. Work to improve sanitation in your area by organizing cleaning drives. Ensure clean water by petitioning authorities for better water supply. Create support networks for pregnant women and pool resources to create an emergency transport fund.

To protect future generations, educate your daughters about their bodies and health rights. Support girls' education because educated women have healthier families. Work to break the cycle of early marriage by ensuring girls are 18 or older before marriage. Promote family planning because spacing children improves health outcomes for everyone.

Priya Decides to Have a Baby

After two years of marriage, Priya and Raj decided they were ready to start a family. They had saved some money, felt emotionally ready, and both wanted children.

Preparing for Pregnancy

Before getting pregnant, Priya learned there were several important steps to take. She stopped using birth control methods and started taking folic acid tablets that her doctor prescribed. She focused on eating healthy, nutritious foods and began exercising regularly but not too heavily. Since she didn't smoke or drink alcohol, she didn't need to worry about stopping those habits. She made sure her vaccinations were up to date.

The best age for pregnancy is generally between 20-30 years, which is safest for both mother and baby. It's important to wait until after 18 years old when the body is fully developed, and ideally before 35 years old to have lower risk of complications.

To time pregnancy, Priya learned to track her menstrual cycle. She was most likely to get pregnant around day 14 of her cycle. Her doctor advised having intercourse every 2-3 days around this time. She learned not to stress if it didn't happen immediately, as it can take several months even for healthy couples.

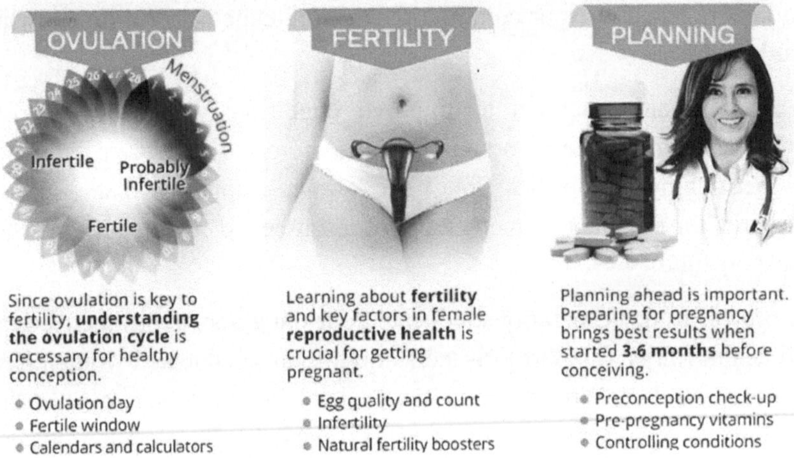

Pic 44: https://www.shecares.com/

Signs of Early Pregnancy

After three months of trying, Priya noticed some changes in her body. The most obvious sign was a missed period. She also felt nauseous, especially in the morning, and her breasts felt tender and bigger. She experienced extreme tiredness and needed to urinate more often than usual. Food smells started making her feel sick, and she noticed mood changes.

To confirm pregnancy, she could use a home pregnancy test available at the pharmacy, get a blood test at a clinic or hospital, or have an examination by a doctor. When Priya's period was two weeks late, she took a pregnancy test. It was positive! She was both excited and nervous.

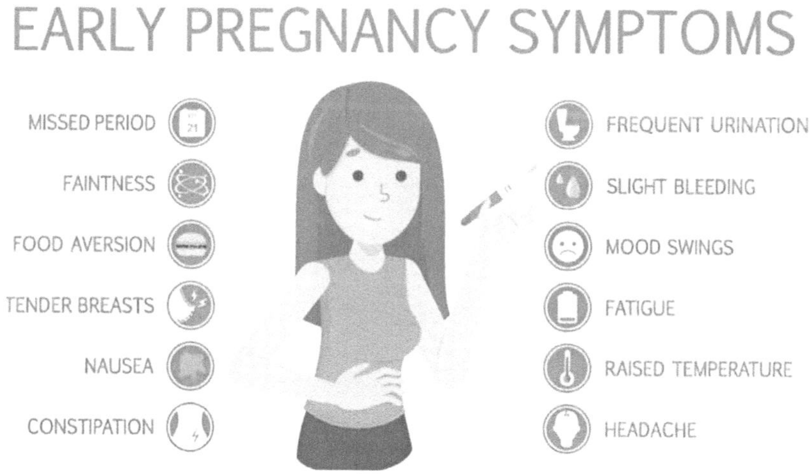

Pic 45: https://www.femina.in/

Priya's Pregnancy Journey

First Three Months (First Trimester)

Priya immediately visited the doctor for confirmation and to start prenatal care. During this time, her baby started as a tiny cell, and the heart began beating around 6 weeks. All major organs started forming, and by 12 weeks, the baby was about 3 inches long.

Priya experienced morning sickness with nausea and vomiting, extreme tiredness, breast tenderness, frequent urination, and food aversions where she didn't want certain foods she normally enjoyed.

Important care during this time included taking folic acid tablets daily, eating small frequent meals, resting when tired, avoiding alcohol, smoking, and unnecessary medicines, and visiting the doctor regularly.

She learned to watch for warning signs including heavy bleeding, severe abdominal pain, persistent vomiting where she couldn't keep food down, high fever, and severe headaches.

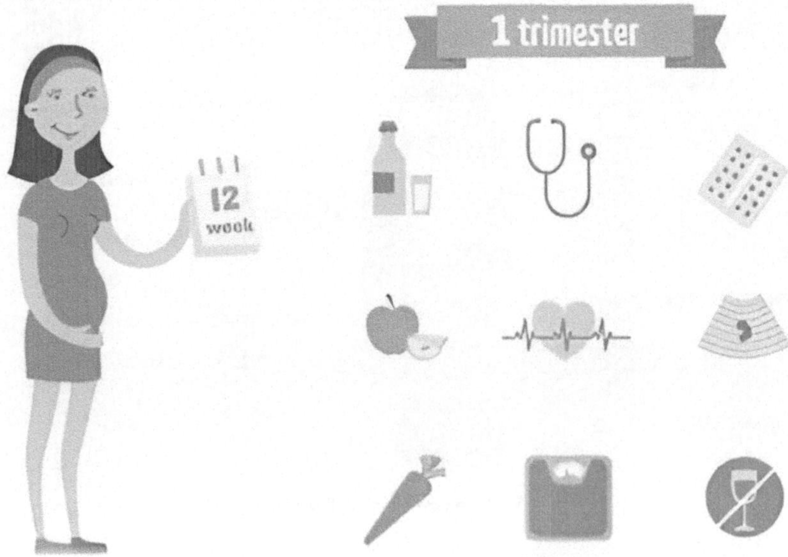

Pic 46: https://www.shutterstock.com/

Second Three Months (Second Trimester)

This was Priya's favorite part of pregnancy because she felt much better and had more energy. During this time, her baby grew rapidly, and she could feel the baby moving around 18- 20 weeks. The baby's sex could be determined, and by 24 weeks, the baby was about 12 inches long.

Priya experienced decreased morning sickness, improved energy levels, the baby's first movements that felt like butterflies, her belly starting to show clearly, and some back pain from the growing belly.

Important care included continuing prenatal vitamins, eating iron-rich foods, doing gentle exercise like walking, wearing comfortable supportive clothes, and sleeping on her side with the left side being best.

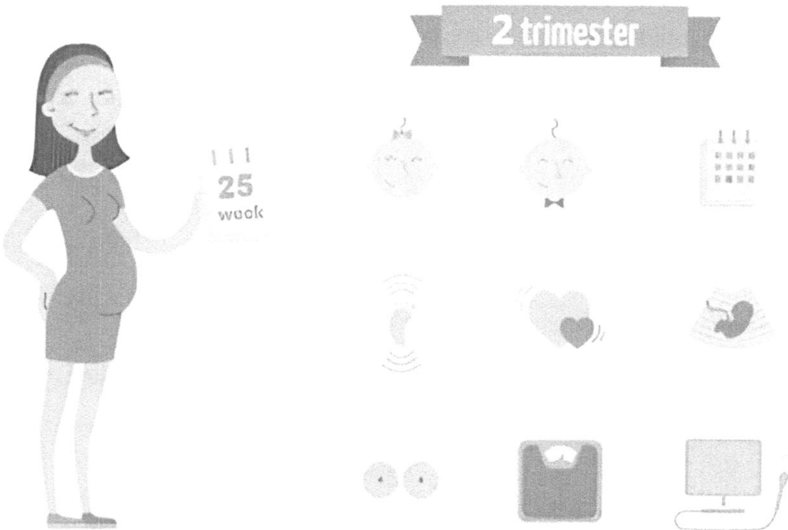

Pic 47: https://www.shutterstock.com/

Tests during this time included ultrasounds to check the baby's growth, blood tests for anemia and other conditions, blood pressure checks, and urine tests.

Last Three Months (Third Trimester)

Priya's belly was now quite large, and she was preparing for delivery. During this time, her baby grew quickly and gained weight, the lungs matured for breathing, and the baby moved into a head-down position, ready to be born.

Priya felt heavy and uncomfortable, had difficulty sleeping, experienced heartburn which is a burning feeling in the chest, had swelling in her feet and hands, felt strong baby movements, and experienced practice contractions called Braxton Hicks.

To prepare for delivery, she chose where to deliver (hospital or birth center), packed her bag for the hospital, learned about labor signs, prepared baby clothes and supplies, and discussed her delivery plan with her doctor.

Pic 48: https://www.shutterstock.com/

Understanding Labor and Delivery

As Priya's due date approached, her mother and doctor taught her about what to expect during labor.

Signs of Labor

Safe Delivery Explained

Priya sat in the clinic, listening carefully as the doctor spoke about childbirth. The doctor smiled warmly and said, "Priya, every woman's delivery can be different, but the important thing is to plan ahead and know what to expect. Let me explain to you in simple words."

Types of Delivery

1. Normal Vaginal Delivery

"This is the most common type. The baby comes out through the birth canal naturally. For most healthy women, this is the safest and simplest way. Sometimes, medicines may be given to help the pains come faster or stronger."

Pic 49: https://www.shutterstock.com/

2. Assisted Vaginal Delivery

"Sometimes, labor may be long, or the baby may need a little help coming out. In such cases, doctors may use safe tools like a vacuum cup or forceps. These are used carefully to guide the baby out. It is only done when absolutely necessary and always under sterile conditions."

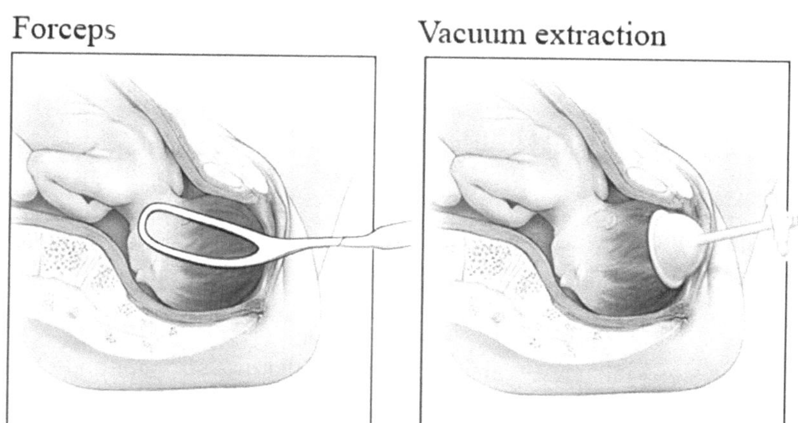

Pic 50: https://www.commonspirit.org/

3. Cesarean Section (C-Section)

"At times, delivery cannot happen safely through the birth canal. Maybe the baby is lying sideways, the mother has very high blood pressure, or there are signs of danger. In such cases, we do a small operation in the mother's abdomen and womb to bring out the baby. This is called a cesarean section. Many mothers recover well after this, though it takes more time than a normal delivery."

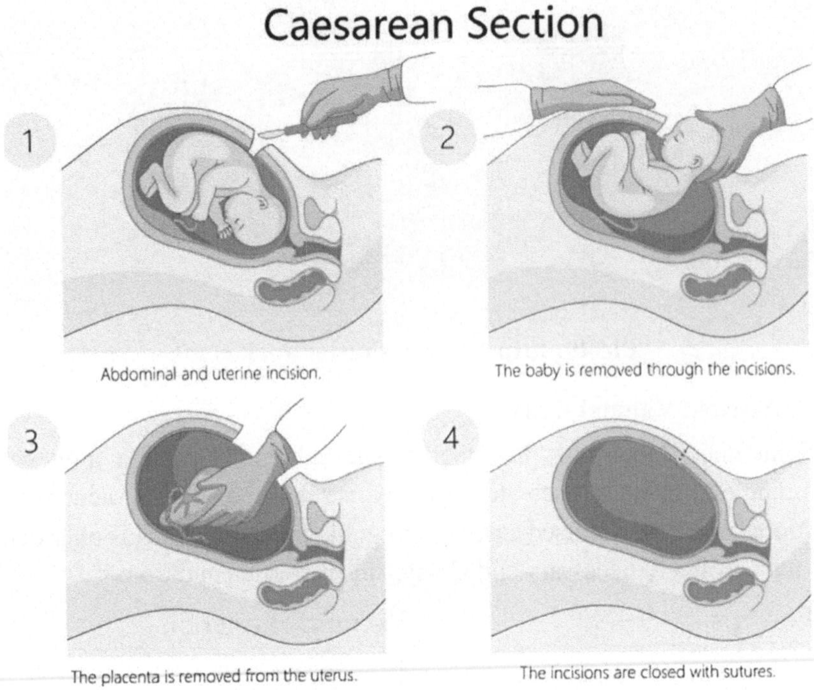

Pic 51: https://thegyneclinic.com/

4. Preterm Delivery

"Sometimes the baby comes before the due date. If this happens, special care is needed because small babies may have trouble breathing, feeding, or fighting infections. Doctors keep a close watch in such cases."

True labor signs include regular contractions that get stronger and closer together, water breaking which is fluid coming from the vagina, bloody show which is a small amount of blood and mucus, and contractions that don't stop when you rest or change position.

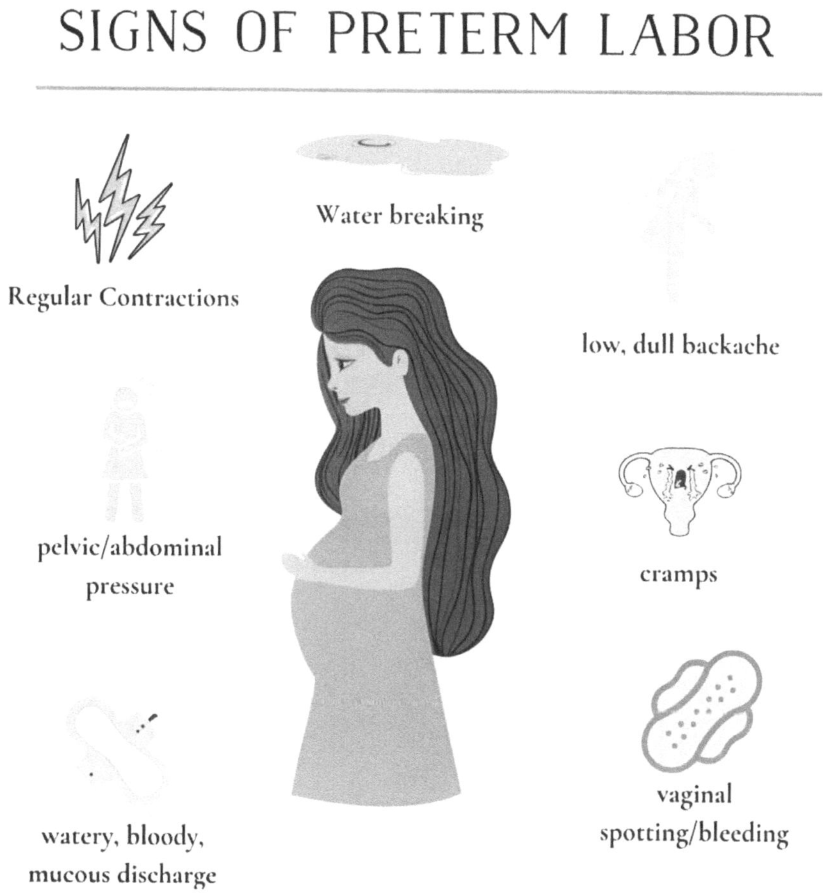

Pic 52: https://www.instagram.com/p/CfZ2ZsUlvec/

You should go to the hospital when contractions come every 5 minutes for an hour, when your water breaks, if you have heavy bleeding, if you experience severe pain, or if you feel worried about something.

Stages of Labor

The first stage has two parts. Early labor involves contractions starting and the cervix opening. This can last 12-20 hours for a first baby. During this time, you can stay at home until contractions are closer together. It's important to rest, eat light foods, and stay hydrated.

Active labor happens when contractions become stronger and closer, coming every 3-5 minutes. This is the time to go to the hospital. The cervix opens from 4-10 centimeters, and you should use breathing techniques for pain management.

The second stage is pushing. This happens when the cervix is fully open. You push when you feel the urge, the baby moves down and is born. This usually takes 30 minutes to 3 hours.

The third stage is delivery of the afterbirth. The placenta comes out, usually within 5-30 minutes. The doctor checks that everything is complete.

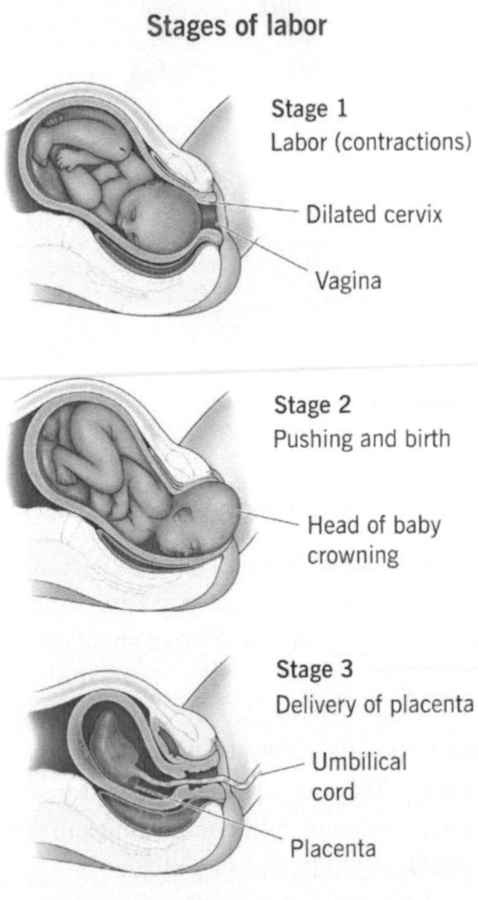

Pic 53: https://my.clevelandclinic.org/

Pain Management

Natural methods include deep breathing techniques, walking during early labor, taking a warm shower or bath, getting massage, and changing positions frequently.

Medical pain relief options include local anesthesia for stitches, epidural which is an injection in the back for pain relief, and pain medications if needed.

After the Baby is Born (Postpartum Care)

Priya successfully delivered a healthy baby girl. Now she needed to learn about caring for herself after delivery.

Immediate After-Birth Care

Physically, Priya experienced bleeding from her vagina for 2-6 weeks called lochia, her uterus slowly shrank back to normal size, her breasts produced milk for feeding the baby, she had stitches from tears during delivery, and she felt tired and emotional.

Warning signs after delivery that require immediate attention include heavy bleeding where you're soaking more than one pad per hour, large blood clots, severe abdominal pain, fever over 100.4°F (38°C), severe headache, difficulty breathing, and signs of infection in stitches.

Pic 54: https://drmadhugoel.com/

Breastfeeding

Priya decided to breastfeed her baby, as recommended by her doctor. Breastfeeding provides perfect nutrition for the baby, protects the baby from infections, helps the mother's uterus return to normal size, reduces the mother's risk of certain cancers, saves money on formula, and creates a special bond with the baby.

To get started, begin breastfeeding within the first hour after birth, feed the baby 8-12 times per day, let the baby nurse on one breast until finished then offer the other breast, and burp the baby after feeding.

Common challenges include sore nipples which usually improve in the first week, feeling like you don't have enough milk, the baby seeming hungry all the time, and engorged breasts that are too full and painful.

Solutions include making sure the baby is latching correctly, feeding frequently to build milk supply, applying warm compresses for engorgement, and asking for help from experienced women or lactation consultants.

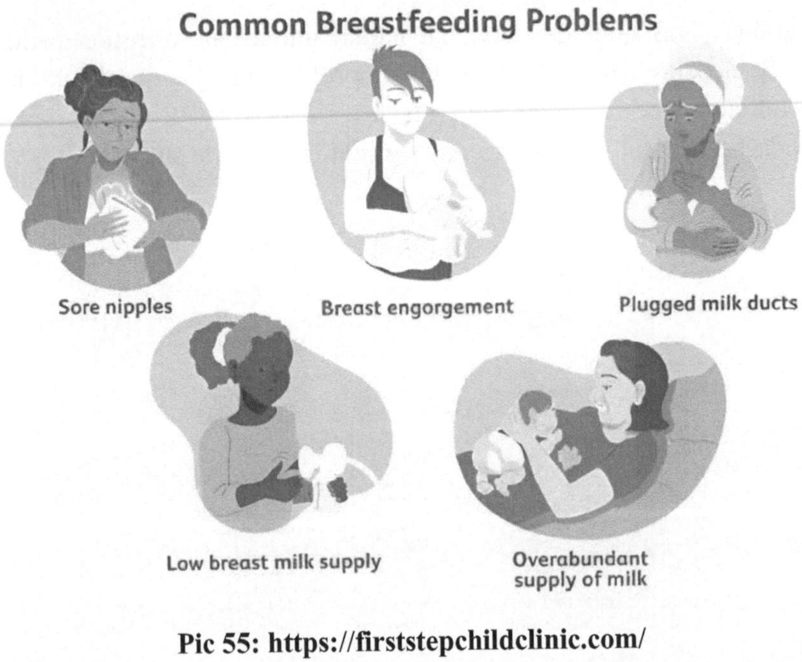

Pic 55: https://firststepchildclinic.com/

Emotional Changes after Birth

Baby blues involve feeling sad, anxious, or overwhelmed, crying for no reason, mood swings, and difficulty sleeping even when the baby sleeps. This usually lasts 1-2 weeks after birth and is completely normal.

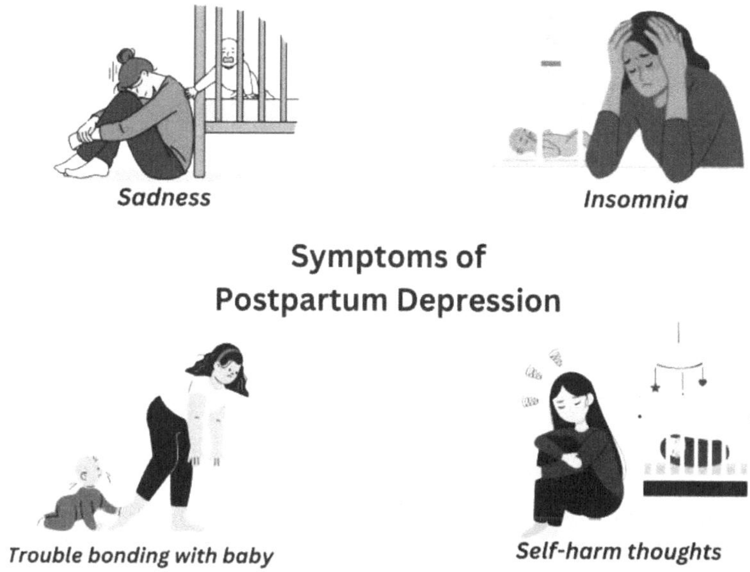

Pic 56: https://click2pro.com/blog/postpartum-depression-signs-support-thane

Postpartum depression is more serious and requires attention when feelings last more than 2 weeks, you feel like you can't care for your baby, you have thoughts of hurting yourself or your baby, you have no interest in your baby or activities, or you experience severe anxiety or panic attacks.

Getting help involves talking to family members about your feelings, seeing a doctor if symptoms are severe, joining support groups for new mothers, and accepting help from family and friends.

Family Planning After Birth

Priya and Raj wanted to wait before having another baby, so they discussed family planning options.

When Fertility Returns

Breastfeeding delays the return of periods, but you can get pregnant before your first period returns. If you're not breastfeeding, periods may return in 6-8 weeks. If you're breastfeeding exclusively, you may not have periods for several months.

Safe Contraception While Breastfeeding

Safe options include condoms, progestin-only pills called mini-pills, IUDs, injectable contraceptives, and the lactational amenorrhea method if you're exclusively breastfeeding. You should avoid combined birth control pills because they can reduce milk supply.

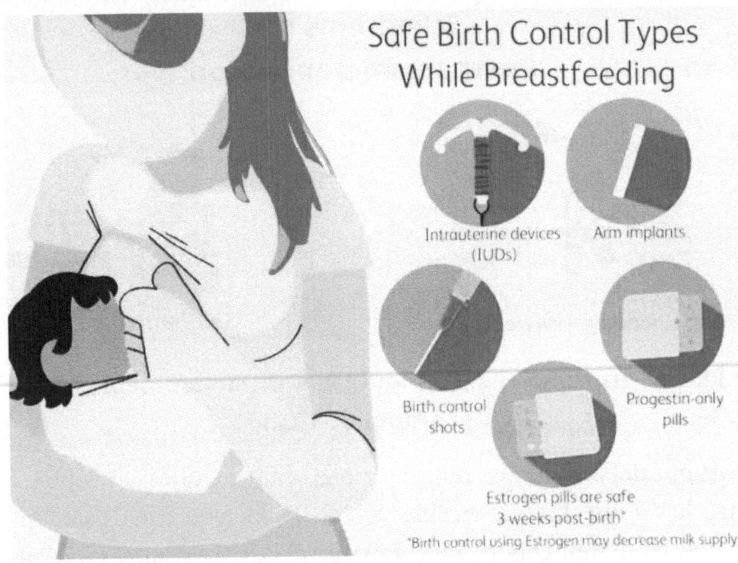

Pic 57: https://www.verywellhealth.com/

Spacing between Pregnancies

It's recommended to wait at least 18 months between pregnancies, with ideal spacing being 2-3 years between pregnancies. This allows the body to recover fully and reduces the risk of complications in the next pregnancy.

Common Pregnancy Complications

Priya was fortunate to have a healthy pregnancy, but her doctor had educated her about possible complications to watch for.

High Blood Pressure in Pregnancy

High blood pressure in pregnancy means blood pressure higher than 140/90. It can develop at any time during pregnancy and can be dangerous for both mother and baby.

Symptoms include severe headaches, vision changes such as seeing spots or blurry vision, swelling in face and hands, pain under right ribs, and sudden weight gain.

Prevention involves attending all prenatal appointments, eating a healthy diet with less salt, exercising as recommended by your doctor, and taking prescribed medications.

Gestational Diabetes

Gestational diabetes is high blood sugar during pregnancy. It usually develops in the second half of pregnancy and often goes away after delivery.

Risk factors include family history of diabetes, previous large baby over 9 pounds, being overweight, and age over 25.

Symptoms include excessive thirst, frequent urination, fatigue, and blurred vision.

Management involves following a special diet, monitoring blood sugar, exercising as approved by your doctor, and possibly needing insulin injections.

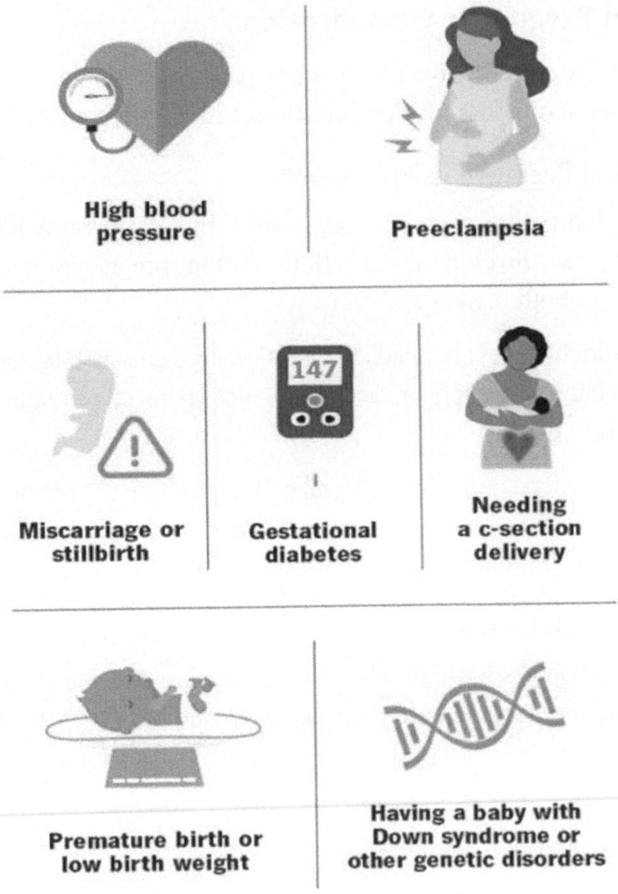

Pic 58: https://my.clevelandclinic.org/

Anemia in Pregnancy

Anemia is common in pregnancy because the body needs more iron for the growing baby, blood volume increases during pregnancy, and many women don't eat enough iron- rich foods.

Symptoms include extreme fatigue, pale skin, nails, or inner eyelids, shortness of breath, dizziness, and cold hands and feet.

Prevention and treatment involve taking iron supplements as prescribed, eating iron-rich foods like green leafy vegetables, beans, and meat, eating vitamin C foods to help iron absorption, and cooking in iron pots when possible.

Infections during Pregnancy

Urinary tract infections are more common during pregnancy and can lead to kidney infection if untreated. Symptoms include burning urination, frequent urination, and pelvic pain.

Vaginal infections, particularly yeast infections, are common during pregnancy. Symptoms include itching and unusual discharge. Safe treatments are available during pregnancy.

Prevention involves drinking plenty of water, urinating frequently, wiping from front to back, wearing cotton underwear, and keeping the genital area clean and dry.

Miscarriage

Miscarriage is the loss of pregnancy before 20 weeks. It's most common in the first 12 weeks and is often due to chromosomal problems in the baby.

Symptoms include vaginal bleeding, cramping or abdominal pain, passing tissue from the vagina, and sudden disappearance of pregnancy symptoms.

Risk factors include advanced maternal age over 35, previous miscarriages, certain medical conditions, and smoking or alcohol use.

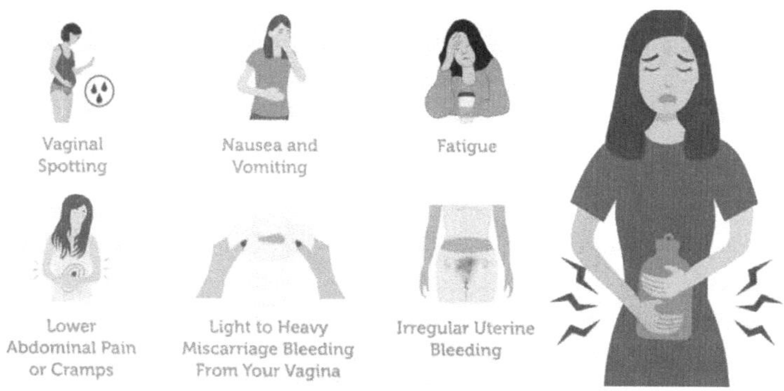

Pic 59: https://www.lybrate.com/

It's important to know that most miscarriages cannot be prevented and it's not the mother's fault. Most women who have a miscarriage go on to have healthy pregnancies. Emotional support is important for healing.

Pregnancy and the Early Months – A Delicate Journey

When Priya became pregnant, she was filled with happiness and a sense of responsibility. But her grandmother reminded her, “Pregnancy is like carrying a flower bud—it needs protection and care until it blossoms.”

The first three months, known as the **first trimester**, are the most delicate. This is when the baby’s organs begin to form, and the mother’s body works hard to adjust. Priya was careful to follow the advice of her elders and health workers during this period.

A Childhood Friend’s Miscarriage

One day, Priya visited her childhood friend, Meena, who lived in the next lane of their neighborhood. Meena had recently suffered a miscarriage. She looked pale and weak, and her eyes were full of sadness. Priya sat beside her, holding her hand.

Meena whispered, “I thought I was going to be a mother. But suddenly, I started bleeding heavily, and the baby was gone. I don’t know what I did wrong.”

Priya’s grandmother, who had accompanied her, comforted Meena gently. “Child, this is not your fault. Miscarriages are common, especially in the first three months. Sometimes the baby does not grow properly, sometimes nature decides it is not the right time. Lifting a bucket of water or walking fast does not cause this. Do not blame yourself.”

Pic 60: https://www.lybrate.com/

Warning Signs in the First Trimester

The neighbourhood health worker also came to check on Meena. She explained, "It is important for all women to know the warning signs in early pregnancy. Heavy bleeding, passing clots, strong cramping or abdominal pain, sudden loss of pregnancy symptoms, fever with foul-smelling discharge, or severe dizziness should never be ignored. If these happen, go to a health center immediately."

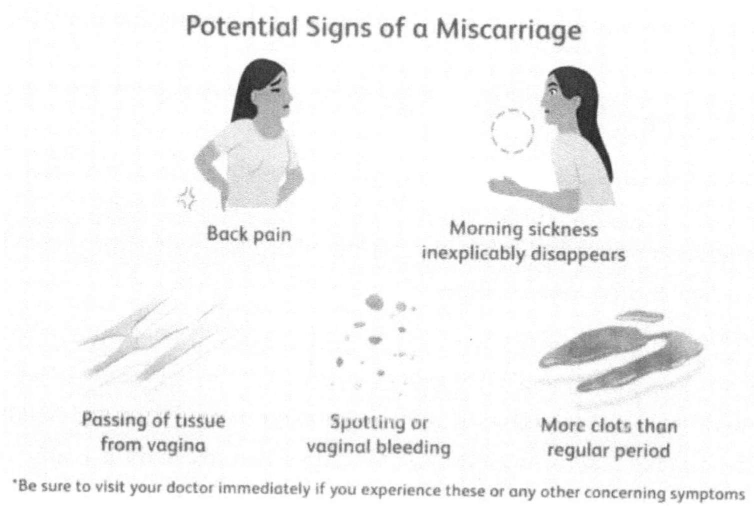

Pic 61: https://www.parents.com/

She reassured the women gathered around, "A little spotting can be normal, but heavy bleeding is not. Always listen to your body—it gives signals when something is wrong."

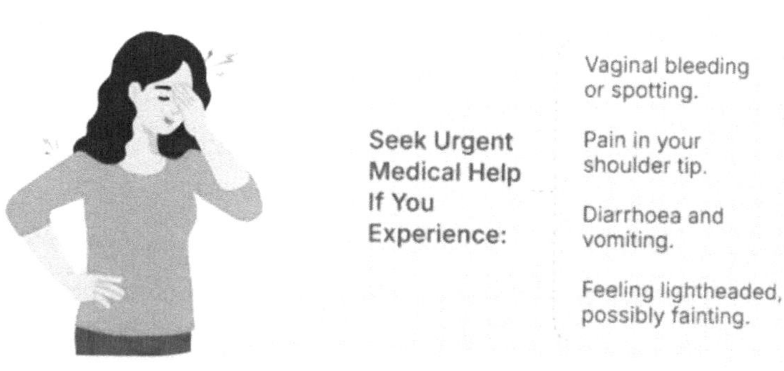

Pic 62: https://www.apollopharmacy.in/

Healing after Miscarriage

Meena needed both physical and emotional healing. The health worker advised her to rest, eat iron- and protein-rich food, and continue taking folic acid tablets to rebuild strength. She also told her family, "Do not let Meena feel guilty. Support her. She can have a healthy pregnancy in the future. One miscarriage does not mean she cannot become a mother."

The women in the neighbourhood shared their own stories— some had also faced miscarriages but later had children. Hearing this gave Meena hope.

Emotional Recovery

Priya noticed that Meena often sat quietly, staring into space. Her aunt reminded everyone, "Loss brings sadness, but silence makes it worse. Encourage her to talk, let her cry, let her share her pain. She needs love and understanding, not loneliness."

Slowly, with the care of her family and friends, Meena regained her strength. She smiled again, though her eyes still carried traces of sorrow. She told Priya one evening, "I now understand that miscarriage is not the end. I will take care of myself and try again when my body is ready."

Priya held her friend's hand tightly and said, "You are strong, Meena. We are all with you."

Understanding Why Miscarriages Happen

When the women in the neighborhood gathered around Meena, many of them asked the health worker, "Why does miscarriage happen? Did she do something wrong?"

The health worker shook her head. "No, most miscarriages are not because of anything a woman did. They are usually caused by natural reasons that no one can control." She explained carefully, so that everyone could understand:

- **Problems in the baby's chromosomes**: Sometimes the baby's building blocks, called genes, do not form properly. In such cases, the pregnancy cannot continue, and nature ends it on its own.

- **Weakness in the mother's body**: If the mother is very undernourished, severely anemic, or has uncontrolled health conditions like thyroid problems or diabetes, her body may struggle to support the pregnancy.
- **Infections**: Some strong infections, like rubella or severe urinary infections, can disturb the pregnancy.
- **Unhealthy lifestyle**: Smoking, alcohol, or certain drugs increase the risk, though these are less common in poor communities where people already struggle to afford basic things.
- **Problems in the womb**: Rarely, the womb itself may have growths (like fibroids) or an unusual shape, making it difficult for the baby to grow.

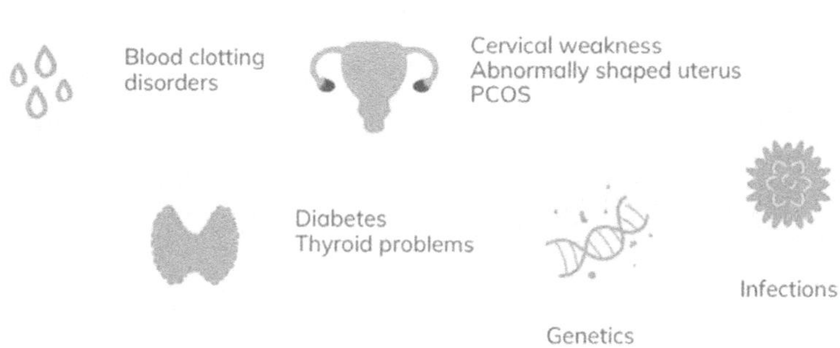

Pic 63: https://miscarriageaustralia.com.au/

The health worker reassured everyone: "Working at home, walking, climbing steps, or lifting light loads usually do not cause miscarriage. So, never blame a woman for losing her baby—it is not her fault."

When Doctors Suggest Medical Abortion

As the conversation continued, one elder woman asked, "If miscarriage happens naturally, why do doctors sometimes do an operation or give medicines to remove the baby?"

The health worker explained patiently, "That is called **medical abortion or medical termination of pregnancy (MTP)**. Doctors recommend it when continuing the pregnancy is dangerous for the mother or when the baby cannot survive."

She listed the common reasons in simple words:

- **Incomplete miscarriage**: Sometimes bleeding starts, but the womb does not empty fully. If the remaining tissue stays inside, it can cause heavy bleeding or infection. In such cases, medicines or a small procedure are needed to clean the womb.
- **Baby not developing**: Sometimes the baby stops growing in the womb but does not come out. This is called a "missed miscarriage." A doctor may advise medicine or a small surgery to remove it safely.
- **Danger to the mother's life**: If the mother has very high blood pressure, severe heart disease, or other health risks, continuing pregnancy can threaten her life. In these cases, medical abortion may be necessary.
- **Serious problems in the baby**: Rarely, scans may show that the baby has major abnormalities and cannot survive outside the womb. In such cases, doctors may suggest ending the pregnancy for the family's well-being.

The health worker emphasized, "Such decisions are never taken lightly. Only trained doctors in approved hospitals or clinics should do this. Never go to an unqualified person for abortion—it can be life-threatening."

Support and Care after Loss

After listening, Meena's mother sighed with relief. She had secretly blamed Meena, thinking she had overworked. Now she realized it was not her daughter's fault. Priya also noticed the change—Meena's family began to support her more, giving her rest, nutritious food, and love.

The health worker ended the visit with kind words: "Every woman deserves care, respect, and medical help when something goes wrong. Miscarriage is painful, but it does not end a woman's dream of becoming a mother. With proper health, most women go on to have healthy babies in the future."

Nutrition during Pregnancy and Breastfeeding

Important Nutrients

Folic acid prevents birth defects of the brain and spine. Take 400-800 mcg daily. It's found in green leafy vegetables, beans, and fortified cereals.

Iron prevents anemia and is needed for the baby's growth. You need 27 mg daily. It's found in meat, beans, spinach, and dried fruits.

Calcium builds the baby's bones and teeth and prevents the mother's bone loss. You need 1000 mg daily. It's found in milk, yogurt, cheese, and green vegetables.

Protein builds the baby's organs and tissues, and mothers need extra protein during pregnancy. It's found in meat, fish, eggs, beans, and dairy products.

Foods to Eat More Of

Eat at least 5 servings of fruits and vegetables per day. Choose a variety of colors to get different vitamins. Fresh, frozen, or canned in water are all good options.

Whole grains like brown rice, whole wheat bread, and oats provide energy and B vitamins and help prevent constipation.

Dairy products including milk, yogurt, and cheese provide calcium and protein. Choose low-fat options when possible.

Protein foods such as lean meat, fish, eggs, beans, and nuts are important for the baby's growth. Fish provides healthy fats for brain development.

Foods to Limit or Avoid

During pregnancy, avoid raw or undercooked meat, eggs, and fish. Avoid high-mercury fish like shark and swordfish. Don't eat unpasteurized dairy products. Avoid alcohol completely as there is no safe amount. Limit caffeine to less than 200mg per day.

During breastfeeding, limit alcohol, and if you do consume any, wait 2-3 hours before breastfeeding. Limit caffeine as it can make babies fussy. Some babies are sensitive to spicy foods in their mother's diet.

Pic 64: https://www.shutterstock.com/

Staying Hydrated

You need 8-10 glasses of water per day during pregnancy and 12-13 glasses per day while breastfeeding. Drink more in hot weather or if exercising.

Signs of good hydration include light yellow urine, feeling energetic, and having moist lips and mouth.

Exercise during Pregnancy

Benefits of Exercise

Exercise during pregnancy reduces back pain and constipation, improves mood and energy, helps with sleep, prepares the body for labor, leads to faster recovery after birth, and reduces the risk of gestational diabetes.

Safe Exercises

Recommended activities include walking, swimming, prenatal yoga, stationary cycling, and low-impact aerobics. heavy weightlifting.

Avoid contact sports, activities with fall risk like skiing and horseback riding, lying flat on your back after the first trimester, and heavy weightlifting

Pic 65: https://www.truworthwellness.com/

Warning Signs to Stop Exercise

Stop exercising immediately if you experience vaginal bleeding, shortness of breath before exercise starts, dizziness or fainting, headache, chest pain, or calf pain or swelling.

Mental Health during Pregnancy and After Birth

Emotional Changes during Pregnancy

Common feelings include excitement mixed with worry, mood swings, concerns about the baby's health, anxiety about parenting, and body image concerns.

Normal responses include crying more easily, feeling overwhelmed sometimes, worrying about the future, and feeling closer to your partner or family.

When to Seek Help

Warning signs include persistent sadness or anxiety, no interest in pregnancy or baby preparations, thoughts of harming yourself, panic attacks, and being unable to function normally.

Getting support involves talking to trusted family members, joining pregnancy support groups, seeing a counselor if needed, and not suffering in silence.

Preparing for Parenthood

What New Parents Need to Know

Baby care basics include learning how to hold and handle a newborn, diaper changing, bathing the baby, recognizing hunger and sleep cues, and knowing when to call the doctor.

Safety considerations include safe sleep practices with back sleeping, proper car seat installation, baby-proofing the home, and recognizing signs of illness.

Support systems should include family members who can help, other new parents for advice, healthcare providers for questions, and community resources.

Planning for the Future

Health considerations include regular check-ups for mother and baby, vaccination schedules for the baby, family planning for future pregnancies, and maintaining the mother's health.

Financial planning involves considering medical expenses, baby supplies and equipment, childcare costs, and potential changes in family income.

Common Illnesses during Pregnancy and Safe Treatment

Illnesses More Common During Pregnancy

Morning sickness and nausea involve feeling sick and vomiting, especially in the morning. This is normal during the first 3 months when it's not severe. You should worry if you can't keep any food or water down for 24 or more hours. Safe treatments include eating small frequent meals, drinking ginger tea, and eating dry crackers. Avoid anti-nausea medicines without a doctor's prescription.

Constipation happens because pregnancy hormones slow digestion. Symptoms include difficulty passing stool, hard stools, and stomach discomfort. Safe treatments include drinking more water, eating fruits and vegetables, and walking daily. Avoid laxative medicines and herbal purgatives.

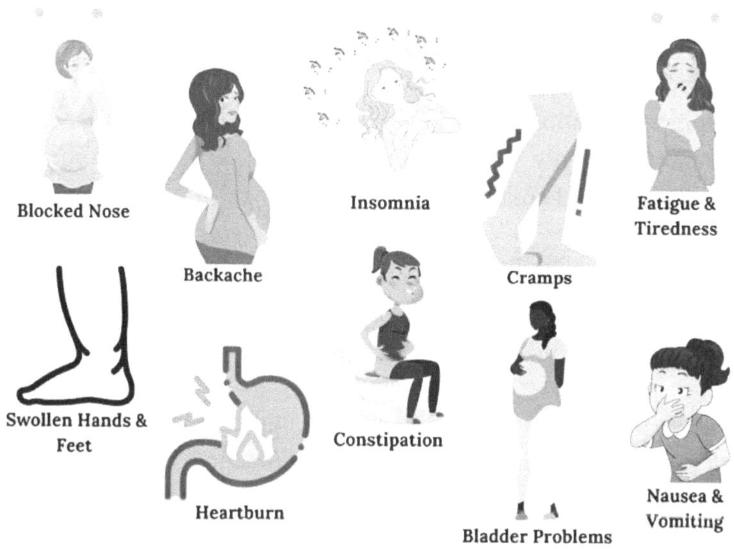

Pic 66: https://feedmomandme.com/

Heartburn causes a burning feeling in the chest, especially after eating. Safe treatments include eating small frequent meals, avoiding spicy foods, and sleeping with your head elevated. Avoid antacid tablets without your doctor's approval.

Haemorrhoids are painful swelling around the anus with bleeding during bowel movements. Safe treatments include eating high fiber foods, drinking water, and taking warm baths. Avoid suppositories or creams without medical advice.

Leg cramps usually happen at night and are more common in later pregnancy. Safe treatments include gentle stretching, warm compresses, and proper foot support. Avoid pain relief medicines without consultation.

Back pain happens because of extra weight and changed posture. Safe treatments include gentle exercise, proper posture, and warm compresses. Avoid pain killers and muscle relaxants.

Swelling in feet and hands is normal when it's mild swelling, especially in the evening. You should worry about sudden severe swelling, especially with headache. Safe treatments include resting with feet up and reducing salt intake. Avoid water pills without prescription.

Skin problems commonly include dark patches, stretch marks, and itchy skin. Safe treatments include gentle moisturizers and avoiding harsh soaps. Avoid steroid creams and whitening creams.

Dangerous Medications During Pregnancy

Regular medicines are dangerous during pregnancy because the baby's organs are developing, especially in the first 3 months when medicines can cause birth defects. Pregnancy changes how the body processes medicines, some can cause miscarriage, others can harm the baby's growth causing low birth weight or developmental problems, and some medicines can complicate delivery.

Common pain killers you should never take without a doctor include aspirin, which can cause bleeding problems and heart defects in the baby. Ibuprofen (Brufen, Combiflam) can harm the baby's kidneys and heart. Stronger pain medicines can cause addiction in the baby. Paracetamol is a safe alternative, but only with doctor's approval.

Pic 67: https://stock.adobe.com/

Dangerous antibiotics include tetracycline, which causes yellow teeth and bone problems in babies. Streptomycin can cause hearing loss in babies. Chloramphenicol can cause serious blood problems. Safe alternatives include only specific antibiotics approved by your doctor.

Stomach medicines to avoid include antacids with aluminum, which can be harmful in large amounts. Laxatives can cause contractions and premature labor. Anti-diarrhea medicines can mask serious infections.

Blood pressure medicines like ACE inhibitors can cause kidney problems in babies. Some water pills can reduce blood flow to the baby. Only specific BP medicines are safe, and your doctor must choose them.

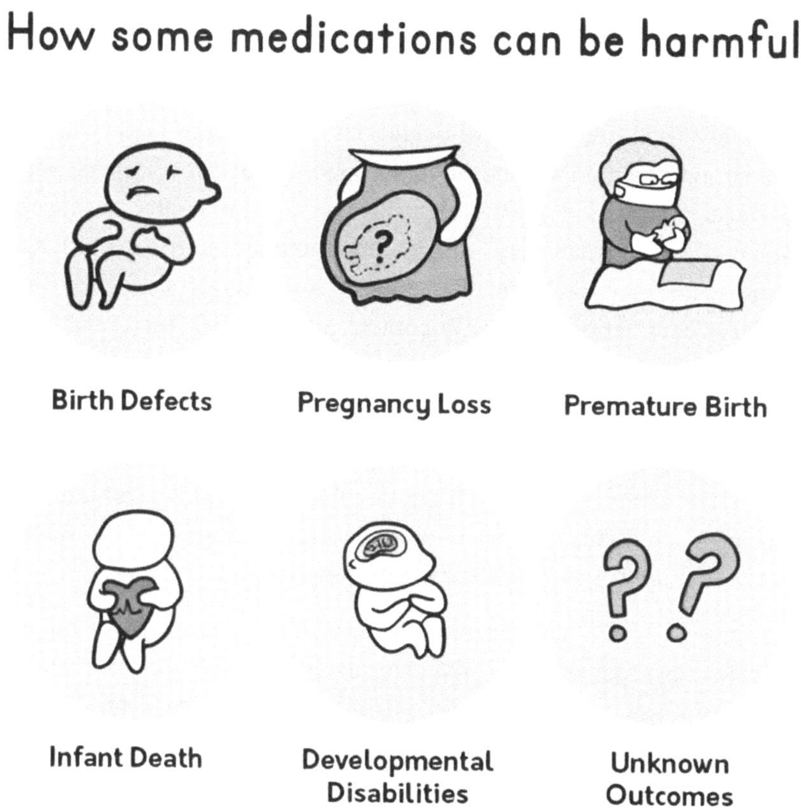

Pic 68: https://www.erufucare.com/

Most oral diabetes medicines can cause low blood sugar in babies. Insulin is usually safer but the dose needs adjustment.

Mental health medicines including most antidepressants need careful evaluation of risks versus benefits. Anxiety medicines can cause withdrawal in babies. Sleeping pills can affect the baby's breathing.

Skin medicines to avoid include acne medicines like Isotretinoin, which cause severe birth defects. Steroid creams can be absorbed and affect the baby. Whitening creams often contain harmful chemicals.

Most cough and cold medicines contain alcohol or harmful ingredients. Decongestants can affect blood flow to the baby. Combination cold medicines often contain multiple harmful ingredients.

Traditional Remedies That Can Be Dangerous

Commonly used herbs that are dangerous include castor oil, which can cause strong contractions and premature labor. Raw or semi-ripe papaya can cause contractions and miscarriage. Large amounts of pineapple contain enzymes that may trigger contractions. Large quantities of sesame seeds may cause bleeding. Large amounts of asafoetida (hing) can cause contractions. Large quantities of fenugreek seeds may cause premature labor.

Dangerous traditional practices include heavy abdominal massage, which can harm the baby or cause placental problems. Consuming alcohol-based tonics harms the baby's brain development. Taking purgatives for cleansing can cause severe dehydration. Using strong smelling substances may trigger nausea or breathing problems.

Metal-based traditional medicines including lead-based kajal or medicines can cause brain damage in babies. Mercury- containing preparations are extremely toxic to developing babies. Iron filings or crude metal preparations can cause poisoning.

Safe Alternatives for Common Problems

For nausea and vomiting, try ginger tea by boiling fresh ginger in water, which is safe in small amounts. Lemon water can help reduce nausea. Eat small frequent meals like crackers and dry toast. Avoid empty stomach and strong smells.

For constipation, eat high fiber foods including vegetables, fruits, and whole grains. Drink plenty of water, at least 8-10 glasses daily. Do gentle exercise as walking helps digestion. Prunes or dates have a natural laxative effect.

For cough and cold, try steam inhalation by breathing steam from hot water. Gargle with warm salt water for sore throat.

Use honey and ginger in small amounts for cough. Rest and fluids help the body fight infection naturally.

For acidity, eat small frequent meals and don't stay hungry. Avoid spicy and oily foods as these increase acidity. Sleep with your head elevated using extra pillows. Cold milk can provide temporary relief.

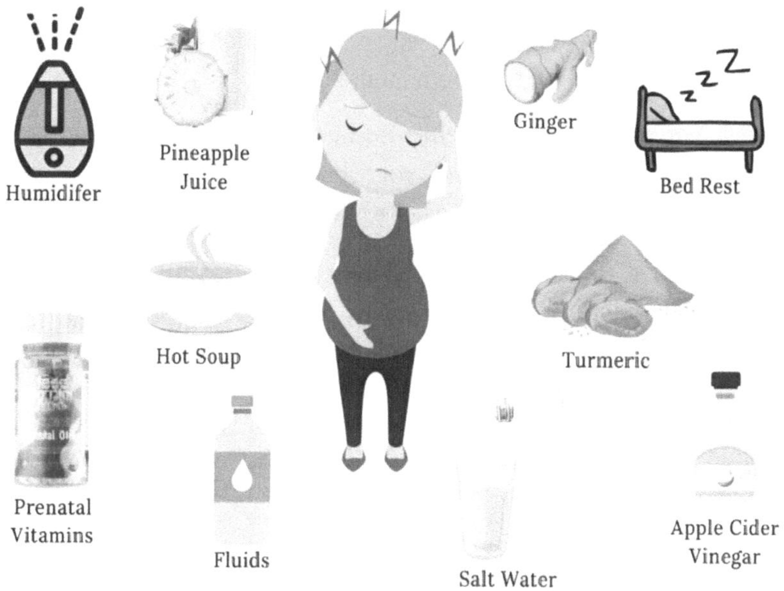

Pic 69: https://feedmomandme.com/

For body aches, use warm compresses with a hot water bag or warm cloth. Get gentle massage by an experienced person, avoiding deep pressure. Rest and don't overexert yourself. Maintain proper posture and avoid slouching.

Why Doctor Consultation is Essential

Every woman's body is different, so what's safe for one woman may not be safe for another. Your medical history affects what medicines you can take, and other health conditions change what's safe during pregnancy.

Pregnancy changes everything. Medicines that were safe before pregnancy may become dangerous. Dose adjustments are needed even for safe medicines. The timing of medication matters in pregnancy.

The baby's development stages are important because different medicines are dangerous at different stages. The first 3 months, when organs are forming, many medicines cause birth defects. In later pregnancy, some medicines affect growth and delivery.

Hidden interactions can be dangerous. Medicines can interact with each other dangerously. Food and medicine interactions occur. Traditional remedies can interact with modern medicines.

Professional assessment is needed because doctors can weigh benefits versus risks, monitor you and your baby for any problems, adjust treatment as pregnancy progresses, and provide safer alternatives.

What to Do When You're Sick During Pregnancy

First, don't self-medicate. Resist the urge to take your usual medicines. Don't ask the pharmacist for "pregnancy-safe" medicines. Don't rely on advice from friends or family about medicines.

Second, try safe home remedies first. Use rest and fluids for minor illnesses. Make simple dietary changes. Use non- medicinal comfort measures.

Third, know when to see a doctor immediately. This includes high fever over 101°F, persistent vomiting, severe pain anywhere, difficulty breathing, and signs of infection.

Fourth, be honest with your doctor. Tell about all medicines you've taken. Mention traditional remedies you've used. Share all symptoms, even if embarrassing. Ask about the safety of any medicines prescribed.

Pic 70: https://stock.adobe.com/

Fifth, follow medical advice completely. Take prescribed medicines exactly as directed. Complete the full course of antibiotics if prescribed. Don't stop medicines early even if feeling better. Report any side effects immediately.

Emergency Situations Requiring Immediate Medical Care

Signs of medicine poisoning include severe nausea and vomiting after taking any medicine, difficulty breathing, rapid heartbeat, dizziness or fainting, and skin rash or swelling.

Signs of dangerous interactions include unusual bleeding, severe abdominal pain after taking medicines, changes in vision, severe headache, and confusion or unusual behavior.

What to do in these situations: stop all non-essential medicines immediately, go to the nearest hospital, bring medicine bottles or packages with you, and tell medical staff everything you've taken.

Prevention is better than Treatment

To boost natural immunity, eat a variety of fruits and vegetables, get adequate rest and sleep, drink plenty of clean water, practice good hygiene, and avoid sick people when possible.

Prevent common infections by washing hands frequently, cooking food thoroughly, avoiding street food during pregnancy, keeping immunizations up to date, and using mosquito protection.

Manage stress by practicing relaxation techniques, getting support from family and friends, doing light exercise as approved by your doctor, and getting adequate sleep.

Regular prenatal care involves attending all scheduled check- ups, taking prescribed vitamins and supplements, monitoring blood pressure and weight, and getting recommended tests done on time.

Post-Pregnancy Care and Recovery

After Priya delivered her healthy baby girl, she learned that taking care of herself was just as important as taking care of her new baby. The first few months after delivery are crucial for a woman's health and recovery.

Immediate Care after Delivery (First 24-48 Hours)

Your body goes through several changes immediately after delivery. You will experience heavy bleeding like a very heavy period for the first few days, called lochia. Your uterus will shrink back to normal size, causing cramping pain. Your breasts will change as milk production starts, and they may feel full and tender. If you had an episiotomy or tears during delivery, you'll have stitches that need to heal. You'll also feel extremely tired, which is normal after the hard work of labor.

Normal recovery signs include bright red bleeding that gradually decreases, mild to moderate cramping especially while breastfeeding, breasts feeling full but not extremely painful, some pain from stitches that improves daily, and feeling emotional with happiness, sadness, or feeling overwhelmed.

Warning signs that require immediate help include heavy bleeding where you're soaking more than one large pad per hour for 2 or more hours, large blood clots bigger than a lemon, severe abdominal pain that's much worse than normal cramping, high fever over 100.4°F (38°C), severe headache with vision changes or swelling, difficulty breathing or chest pain, signs of infection like red, swollen, hot areas around stitches, or being unable to urinate or having burning pain while urinating.

Physical Recovery in the First Six Weeks

During the first week or two, you can expect bleeding that's still heavy but decreasing, with color changing from red to brown. You'll have pain from stitches and cramping during breastfeeding. Your breasts will be adjusting to milk production and may leak milk. Your energy will be very low, and you'll need lots of rest. Emotionally, mood swings and "baby blues" are common.

In weeks three and four, bleeding becomes much lighter and may be yellowish or white discharge. Stitches should be healing well, and your breasts will be more comfortable with the feeding routine. Your energy will gradually improve, though sleep will still be disrupted by the baby's feeding schedule.

By weeks five and six, bleeding should be minimal or stopped.

Your physical strength will be returning gradually, and your emotional state should be stabilizing. The important 6-week doctor visit will check your recovery progress.

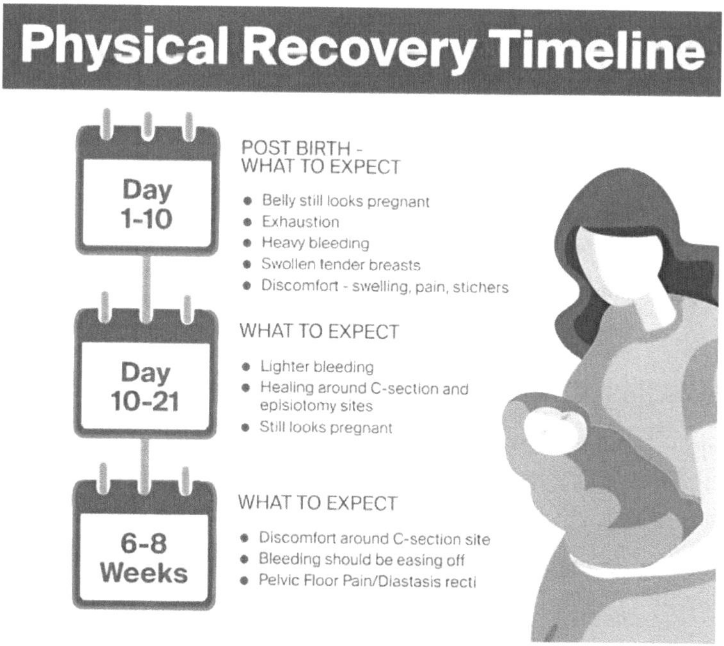

Pic 71: https://www.kennedyjohnson.com/

Care of Stitches and Healing

If you have stitches, keep the area clean by washing with plain water after using the toilet. Pat the area dry rather than rubbing it. Change pads frequently to prevent infection. Wear loose clothing because tight clothes can cause pain. Avoid heavy lifting as this can cause stitches to open.

Watch for signs of infection including a red, swollen area around stitches, increasing pain instead of decreasing pain, pus or bad-smelling discharge, opening of stitches, and fever.

Natural healing aids include warm baths, which can help with comfort and healing. Ice packs for the first few days can reduce swelling. Let the area air dry when possible.

Postpartum Bleeding - What's Normal and What's Not

Normal bleeding follows a pattern. Days 1-3 involve bright red, heavy bleeding like a heavy period. Days 4-10 show red to brown, moderate flow. Days 10-14 have brown to yellow, light flow. Weeks 3-6 show light pink or white discharge.

Bleeding may increase with physical activity, breastfeeding (which causes uterus to contract), standing for long periods, and not getting enough rest.

Dangerous bleeding that requires hospital care includes soaking a large pad every hour for more than 2 hours, blood clots larger than a lemon, bright red bleeding returning after it had slowed down, bleeding with severe pain that doesn't respond to rest, and foul-smelling discharge with bleeding.

Breastfeeding Challenges and Solutions

Common problems in underserved community areas include sore or cracked nipples caused by the baby not latching properly or too much washing with soap. Solutions include checking the baby's position, using only water to clean, and applying breast milk to nipples after feeding. You should worry if nipples are bleeding heavily or showing signs of infection.

Not having enough milk shows signs like the baby crying frequently, not gaining weight, and having very few wet diapers. Solutions include feeding more frequently, drinking more water, eating nutritious food, and getting more rest. Giving water or other foods to babies under 6 months doesn't work and can be harmful.

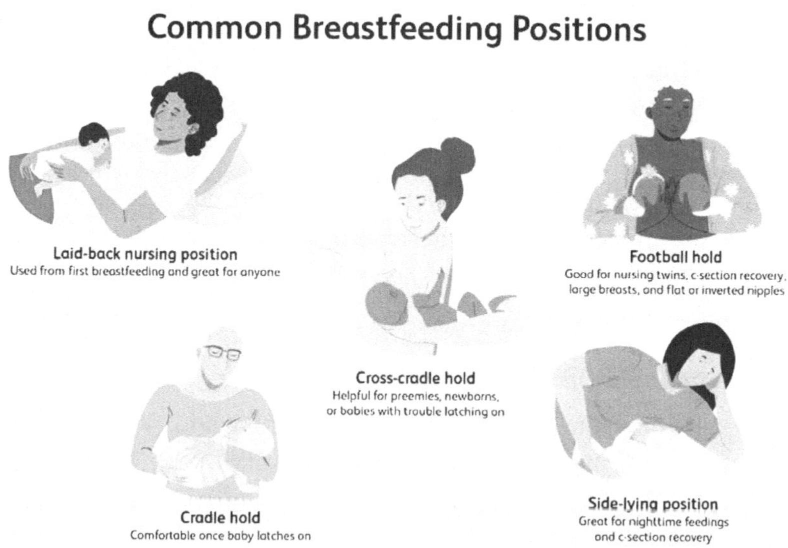

Pic 72: https://www.parents.com/

Too much milk (engorgement) makes breasts very hard and painful, and the baby can't latch properly. Solutions include feeding the baby frequently, expressing some milk by hand, and applying warm compresses before feeding. Cold compresses after feeding provide relief.

Blocked milk ducts create hard, painful lumps in the breast, and skin may be red. Solutions include massaging gently, applying heat, and continuing to feed from the affected breast. You should worry if this is accompanied by fever or red streaks on the skin.

Breast infection (mastitis) causes fever, chills, breast that's hot and red, and feeling very sick. See a doctor immediately for antibiotics, continue breastfeeding, and get rest. Don't stop breastfeeding as it makes the infection worse.

Proper Breastfeeding Technique

For correct position, the baby's body should face your body, not just the head turned. The baby's nose should be level with your nipple. Your hand supports the breast, not pushing the baby's head. The baby's mouth should open wide and take most of the areola (dark area), not just the nipple.

Signs of a good latch include the baby's cheeks being rounded, not sucked in, hearing swallowing sounds, the baby seeming calm and satisfied after feeding, and your nipples not hurting during feeding.

The feeding pattern for newborns is 8-12 times per day (every 2-3 hours). Let the baby finish one breast before offering the other. No schedule is needed - feed when the baby shows hunger signs. Night feeding is important for milk supply.

Nutrition during Breastfeeding

You have extra nutritional needs while breastfeeding. You need about 500 extra calories per day, more protein than during pregnancy, at least 12-13 glasses of water daily, and should continue taking iron and vitamins if prescribed.

Best foods for breastfeeding mothers include protein sources like beans, lentils, eggs, milk, and meat if your family eats it. You need more protein than during pregnancy and should include protein at every meal.

Iron-rich foods including green leafy vegetables, beans, and jaggery are important to prevent anemia. Combine these with vitamin C foods for better absorption.

Calcium sources like milk, yogurt, sesame seeds, and green vegetables are needed for your bones and the baby's development. If you don't eat dairy, focus on other calcium sources.

Healthy fats from nuts, seeds, and small amounts of ghee are important for the baby's brain development. Include these in your daily diet but don't overeat.

Eat at least 5 servings of fruits and vegetables daily. They provide vitamins and minerals, and different colors provide different nutrients.

Foods that may cause problems include excessive spicy food, which may make the baby fussy, too much caffeine, which can make the baby irritable, alcohol, which passes into breast milk and should be avoided completely, and strong-flavored foods like garlic and onions, which some babies are sensitive to.

Mental Health after Delivery

Baby blues are normal and usually start 2-3 days after delivery. Symptoms include crying easily, mood swings, feeling overwhelmed, and anxiety about the baby. This usually improves within 2 weeks. What helps includes rest, support from family, and talking about your feelings.

Postpartum depression is more serious and needs treatment. It can start anytime in the first year. Symptoms include feeling sad and hopeless most of the time, no interest in the baby or daily activities, feeling like you're not a good mother, thoughts of hurting yourself or the baby, severe anxiety or panic attacks, inability to sleep even when the baby sleeps, and no appetite or overeating.

Risk factors in underserved community areas include financial stress and poverty, lack of support from family, living in overcrowded conditions, previous mental health problems, difficult delivery or sick baby, and lack of sleep and rest.

Getting help involves not suffering alone and talking to trusted family members, seeing a doctor because mental health problems can be treated, joining mother's groups to connect with other new mothers, accepting help and letting others help with housework and baby care, and getting traditional support from elderly women in the community who can provide guidance.

Warning signs that need immediate help include thoughts of hurting yourself or the baby, hearing voices or seeing things that aren't there, feeling completely disconnected from reality, and being unable to care for yourself or the baby.

Common Health Problems after Delivery

Anaemia (low blood) is common because of blood loss during delivery, breastfeeding demands, and poor diet. Symptoms include extreme tiredness, pale skin, dizziness, and shortness of breath. Treatment includes eating iron-rich foods, taking iron supplements, and treating any ongoing bleeding. Prevention involves continuing iron supplements as prescribed by your doctor.

Urinary problems including difficulty urinating are common in the first few days. Urinary tract infections cause burning sensation and frequent urination. Treatment involves drinking lots of water, not holding urine, and seeing a doctor for infections.

Hemorrhoids cause painful swelling around the anus and bleeding during bowel movements. They're caused by pushing during delivery and constipation. Treatment includes eating high fiber foods, drinking water, taking warm baths, and avoiding straining.

Constipation is caused by pain medications, fear of pain, and less physical activity. Treatment includes eating high fiber foods, drinking lots of water, and doing gentle exercise as you're able. Avoid strong laxatives without doctor's advice.

Hair loss usually occurs 3-6 months after delivery and is caused by hormonal changes. It's a normal part of recovery. What helps includes eating nutritious diet, gentle hair care, and patience. Hair usually returns to normal within 6-12 months.

Joint pain commonly affects the back, knees, and wrists. It's caused by hormonal changes, carrying the baby, and lack of rest. Treatment includes gentle exercise, proper posture, and adequate rest. You should worry about severe pain that interferes with daily activities.

Safe Medications While Breastfeeding

Generally safe medications include paracetamol for pain and fever, most antibiotics (your doctor will choose safe ones), iron supplements which are often needed for anaemia, and vitamins as prescribed.

Medications to avoid include aspirin, which can affect the baby's blood, some antibiotics (your doctor will know which ones to avoid), strong pain medications which can make the baby sleepy, and birth control pills with estrogen which can reduce milk supply.

Always ask your doctor before taking any new medication, traditional remedies, over-the-counter medicines, or supplements.

Family Planning After Birth

If you're not breastfeeding, ovulation can return in 6-8 weeks. If you're breastfeeding exclusively, you may not ovulate for several months. Importantly, you can get pregnant before your first period returns.

Safe contraception while breastfeeding includes progestin- only pills (mini-pills) that don't affect milk supply but must be taken at the same time every day and are available at government health centers. Condoms are safe with no hormones and are easily available, plus they protect from infections. IUDs (Copper-T) can be inserted 6 weeks after delivery, work for many years, and are available at government hospitals. Injectable contraceptives are safe while breastfeeding, given every 3 months, but may reduce milk supply slightly in some women.

Natural methods include LAM (Lactational Amenorrhea Method), which only works if you're exclusively breastfeeding, have no periods, and your baby is under 6 months. The calendar method involves tracking cycles when periods return. The withdrawal method is not very reliable.

Methods to avoid include combined birth control pills that contain estrogen and can reduce milk supply significantly.

Spacing between Pregnancies

It's recommended to wait at least 18 months between birth and the next pregnancy. Ideal spacing is 2-3 years between pregnancies. The benefits include allowing the mother's body to recover completely, better health for the next baby, and easier care for children.

Risks of pregnancies too close together include higher risk of anemia and pregnancy complications for the mother, higher risk of premature birth and low birth weight for the baby, and financial strain with difficulty caring for multiple small children for the family.

Returning to Work and Daily Activities

For physical activities, spend the first 2 weeks doing minimum activity and focusing on rest and feeding the baby. In weeks 3-6, gradually increase light activities but avoid heavy lifting.

After 6 weeks, you can gradually return to normal activities if feeling well.

When returning to work, ideally wait 3-6 months for exclusive breastfeeding. If possible, express milk during breaks for breastfeeding at work. Arrange safe, reliable childcare for the baby.

Pic 73: https://www.bcrwd.store/

For exercise after delivery, do light walking as comfortable for the first 6 weeks. After your doctor's clearance, gradually increase exercise. Benefits include improved mood, increased energy, and help with weight loss. Warning signs to stop include heavy bleeding, pain, and extreme fatigue.

Baby Care Basics for New Mothers

For feeding, practice exclusive breastfeeding for the first 6 months with no water or other foods. Feed 8-12 times per day initially. Growth signs include regular wet diapers, steady weight gain, and the baby being alert when awake.

For sleep safety, always put the baby on their back to sleep. Use a firm mattress with no pillows or blankets. Keep the baby in the same room but not the same bed.

For hygiene, bathe the baby 2-3 times per week initially, then daily once the umbilical cord heals. Clean the diaper area with water and change frequently. Wash your hands before handling the baby.

See a doctor for the baby if there's any fever (any fever in babies under 3 months), feeding problems like not feeding well or excessive crying, breathing issues like fast or difficult breathing, or skin changes like yellow color (jaundice), rash, or signs of infection.

Pic 74: https://kidswayclinic.com/

Long-term Health Considerations

For bone health, continue eating high calcium foods, get some sun exposure daily for vitamin D, and do weight-bearing activities when able.

For mental health, maintain connections with other mothers for ongoing support, take time for yourself when possible for self-care, and watch for signs of depression beyond the first few months.

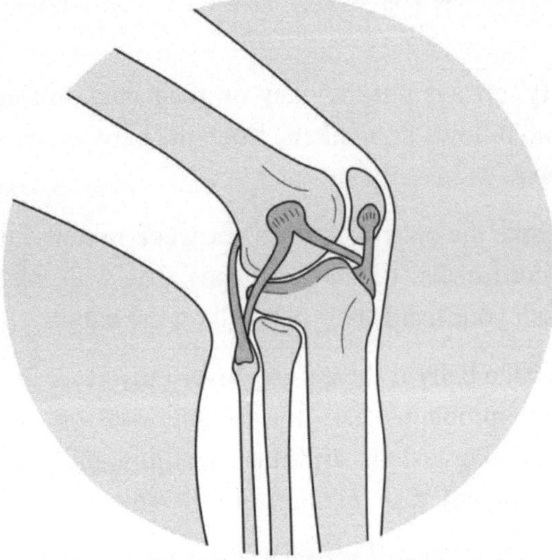

Pic 75: https://www.istockphoto.com/

For reproductive health, resume regular Pap smears as recommended, continue monthly breast self-examinations, and have regular discussions with healthcare providers about family planning.

Special Challenges Some Women Face

Limited privacy for breastfeeding can be addressed by using a dupatta or cloth for covering and finding a quiet corner. Ask other women in the community about private spaces. Don't be discouraged - breastfeeding is natural and important.

Water quality concerns mean ensuring clean drinking water to maintain milk supply for the mother. Use the cleanest water available for personal hygiene. For the baby's safety, give no water under 6 months, even in hot weather.

For healthcare access, use government health services for regular check-up follow-up visits. Know the location of the nearest hospital for emergency care. Build relationships with community health workers and ASHA workers.

Nutrition challenges can be addressed by having the mother eat first to maintain strength. Share resources during difficult times with community support. Access supplementary nutrition programs through government schemes if available.

For work and income, return to work gradually if possible. Arrange safe childcare, often with family members. Plan for reduced income during the recovery period.

When to Resume Sexual Activity

Physical readiness usually occurs after 6 weeks when the doctor clears you at your postpartum visit. Make sure healing is complete with stitches healed and bleeding stopped. Resume when you feel physically and emotionally ready.

Important considerations include using contraception because you can get pregnant before your first period. It may be uncomfortable initially due to hormonal changes, especially while breastfeeding. Communicate openly with your husband about your comfort level. Be patient because recovery takes time, both physical and emotional.

Signs of Good Recovery

Physical signs of good recovery include bleeding that has stopped or is minimal, improving energy levels, ability to care for yourself and your baby, sleeping better when the baby allows, and returned appetite.

Emotional signs include feeling more positive about motherhood, bonding well with your baby, being able to cope with daily challenges, and enjoying some activities again.

When recovery seems slow, don't compare yourself to others because every woman recovers at a different rate. Seek support from family, friends, and healthcare providers. Be patient because full recovery can take 6 months to a year. Ask for help and don't try to do everything alone.

Building a Support Network

For family support, accept help and let family members help with housework and baby care.

Communicate your needs and tell family what kind of help you need most. Share responsibilities - your husband should also help with baby care.

Pic 76: https://stock.adobe.com/

For community support, connect with other mothers to share experiences and advice. Learn from elder women and experienced mothers in the community. Build relationships with nearby families for neighborhood help.

For healthcare support, maintain relationships with healthcare providers through regular check-ups. Ask questions and don't hesitate to ask about any concerns. Know who to call for urgent situations with emergency contacts.

Conclusion: A New Chapter

Priya's journey through marriage and pregnancy taught her many things about her body, her health, and her strength as a woman. She learned that preparation is important because taking care of health before pregnancy leads to better outcomes. Knowledge reduces fear because understanding what to expect makes the experience less scary. Support matters because having family, friends, and healthcare providers helps enormously. Every woman's experience is different, so don't compare your pregnancy to others. Self-care isn't selfish because taking care of yourself helps you take care of your baby.

Key messages for all women include planning your pregnancies when you're ready emotionally and financially.

Get regular prenatal care because it prevents many problems. Eat well and stay active during pregnancy. Ask for help when you need it. Trust your body because it's designed for pregnancy and birth. Take care of your mental health as much as your physical health. Breastfeed if possible because it's best for both mother and baby. Space pregnancies appropriately for better health outcomes.

Marriage and pregnancy are major life changes that require preparation, support, and ongoing care. With the right knowledge and healthcare, most women can have healthy pregnancies and babies. Remember that every pregnancy is unique, and it's important to work with healthcare providers to ensure the best possible outcome for both mother and child.

The journey of becoming a mother is one of the most transformative experiences in a woman's life. Like Priya, with proper preparation, care, and support, you can navigate this journey with confidence and joy.

Chapter - 4
The Next Phase - Perimenopause, Menopause, and Beyond

Priya's Changing Body

Priya was now 45 years old. Her daughter had grown up and was in college. She had been married for over 20 years and felt settled in her life. But recently, she started noticing changes in her body that worried her.

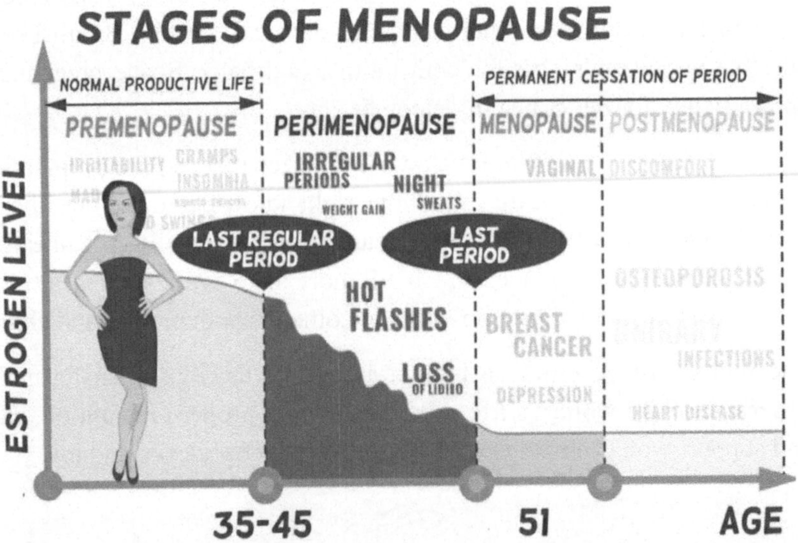

Pic 77: https://www.shutterstock.com/

Her periods, which had been regular for years, started becoming unpredictable. Sometimes they came early, sometimes late. Some months they were very heavy, other months very light. She was also experiencing strange symptoms like sudden hot flashes that made her sweat even when the weather was cool, difficulty sleeping at night, and mood changes that made her feel irritable or sad for no reason.

Priya was confused and scared. She wondered if something was seriously wrong with her. When she talked to her mother and older aunts, they smiled knowingly. "You're entering the change of life," her mother explained gently. "This is normal for women our age. It's called perimenopause, and it means your body is preparing to stop having periods."

Understanding Perimenopause

What Is Perimenopause?

Perimenopause means "around menopause." It's the time when your body slowly transitions from the reproductive years to menopause. This usually starts in your 40s but can begin in your late 30s for some women. During this time, your ovaries gradually produce less estrogen, the hormone that controls your menstrual cycle.

This transition can last anywhere from a few months to 10 years, but it typically takes about 4 years. Your periods may become irregular, but you haven't stopped having them completely yet. You can still get pregnant during perimenopause, so family planning is still important if you don't want more children.

Common Signs and Symptoms

Priya learned that the changes she was experiencing were completely normal. Irregular periods are the most common sign of perimenopause. Your periods may come more frequently or less frequently than before. They may be heavier or lighter than usual. Some months you might skip your period entirely.

Hot flashes are sudden feelings of heat that spread through your body, especially your face, neck, and chest. You may sweat heavily and then feel cold afterward. These can happen during the day or night, disrupting your sleep.

Pic 78: https://www.everydayhealth.com/

Sleep problems become common during this time. You may have trouble falling asleep, staying asleep, or you may wake up very early. Night sweats can wake you up feeling drenched in perspiration.

Mood changes include feeling more irritable, anxious, or sad than usual. You may feel emotionally sensitive or have mood swings that seem to come from nowhere. Some women experience feelings similar to what they felt before their periods when they were younger.

Other physical changes include breast tenderness, decreased interest in sex, vaginal dryness, weight gain especially around the waist, thinning hair, and dry skin. You may also experience headaches, joint aches, and difficulty concentrating or remembering things.

Why These Changes Happen

These symptoms occur because your hormone levels are fluctuating. Estrogen and progesterone, the hormones that control your menstrual cycle, start to decrease and become unpredictable. Your ovaries are slowly reducing their production of these hormones as they prepare to stop releasing eggs.

These hormonal changes affect many parts of your body, not just your reproductive system. Estrogen affects your brain, bones, heart, skin, and many other organs. As levels change, you experience symptoms throughout your body.

Managing Perimenopause Symptoms

There are many ways to manage the symptoms of perimenopause. For irregular periods, keep track of when your periods come and how heavy they are. This information will be helpful when you talk to a doctor. Use appropriate sanitary protection for heavy periods, and don't be surprised if your flow changes from month to month.

For hot flashes, dress in layers so you can remove clothing when you feel hot. Keep your home cool and use fans when possible. Avoid triggers like spicy food, alcohol, caffeine, and stress. Drink cold water when you feel a hot flash starting. Practice deep breathing exercises to help you relax.

To improve sleep, keep your bedroom cool and well- ventilated. Wear lightweight, breathable nightclothes. Avoid caffeine and large meals before bedtime. Try to go to bed and wake up at the same time every day. If night sweats are a problem, keep extra nightclothes and towels near your bed.

For mood changes, get regular exercise, which helps improve mood and reduce stress. Talk to trusted friends or family members about what you're experiencing. Practice relaxation techniques like deep breathing, meditation, or prayer. Don't hesitate to ask for help if you feel overwhelmed.

Maintain a healthy diet by eating plenty of fruits, vegetables, and whole grains. Include foods rich in calcium and vitamin D to support bone health. Limit processed foods, sugar, and excessive salt. Stay hydrated by drinking plenty of water throughout the day.

Menopause - The End of Periods

What Is Menopause?

Menopause officially occurs when you haven't had a period for 12 consecutive months. This usually happens between ages 45 and 55, with the average age being around 51. At this point, your ovaries have stopped releasing eggs and producing most of their estrogen and progesterone.

Menopause is a natural part of aging, not a disease or medical condition. Every woman who lives long enough will experience menopause. It marks the end of your reproductive years, but it doesn't mark the end of your active, healthy life.

Confirming Menopause

You can confirm menopause by tracking your periods. If you haven't had a period for 12 full months and you're in the typical age range, you've reached menopause. Sometimes doctors can do blood tests to check hormone levels, but this isn't always necessary.

It's important to note that if you're taking hormone- containing medications or birth control, these can affect your periods and make it harder to know if you've reached natural menopause. Discuss this with a healthcare provider if you're unsure.

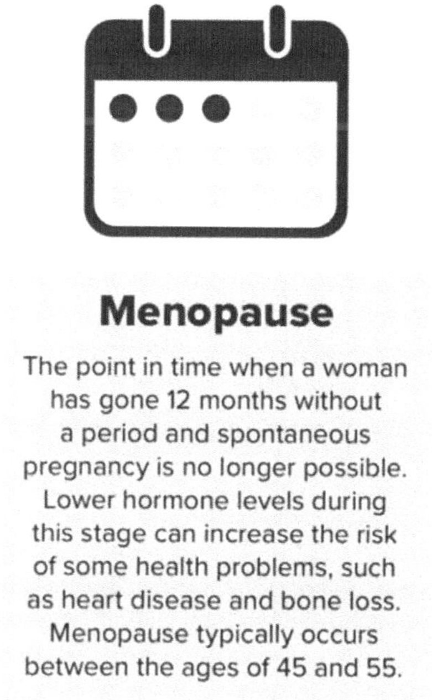

Pic 79: https://womenshealth.gov/nwhw/menopause

Symptoms during Menopause

Many of the symptoms from perimenopause may continue during menopause. Hot flashes often continue and may even become more frequent for some women. Sleep disturbances may persist, and mood changes can continue as your body adjusts to consistently lower hormone levels.

New symptoms may also appear. Vaginal dryness becomes more common as estrogen levels drop, which can make sexual intercourse uncomfortable. Your skin may become drier and thinner. You may notice more joint stiffness and aches.

Some women experience urinary changes, including more frequent urination or urinary tract infections. Memory and concentration problems, sometimes called "brain fog," may become more noticeable.

Pic 80: https://www.freepik.com/

How Long Symptoms Last

The good news is that most menopause symptoms are temporary. Hot flashes typically last for about 2-5 years after your final period, though they can last longer for some women. Other symptoms like mood changes and sleep problems often improve as your body adjusts to its new hormone levels.

Every woman's experience is different. Some women have very mild symptoms that don't interfere with their daily life, while others have more intense symptoms that require treatment. Don't compare your experience to other women's experiences.

Life after Menopause - Post-Menopause

The Post-Menopause Years

Post-menopause refers to all the years after you've completed menopause. This is actually the longest phase of many women's lives, often lasting 30 or more years. While some challenges come with lower hormone levels, many women find this time of life to be fulfilling and freeing.

During post-menopause, your hormone levels remain consistently low. This means that symptoms like hot flashes and mood swings typically improve or disappear entirely. Many women report feeling more stable emotionally and physically during this time.

Health Considerations in Post-Menopause

While many symptoms improve after menopause, the long- term effects of lower estrogen levels create new health considerations. Understanding these helps you take steps to stay healthy and strong in your later years.

Bone health becomes particularly important because estrogen helps maintain bone density. After menopause, women lose bone mass more rapidly, increasing the risk of osteoporosis and fractures. This is why many post-menopausal women are advised to pay special attention to calcium, vitamin D, and weight-bearing exercise.

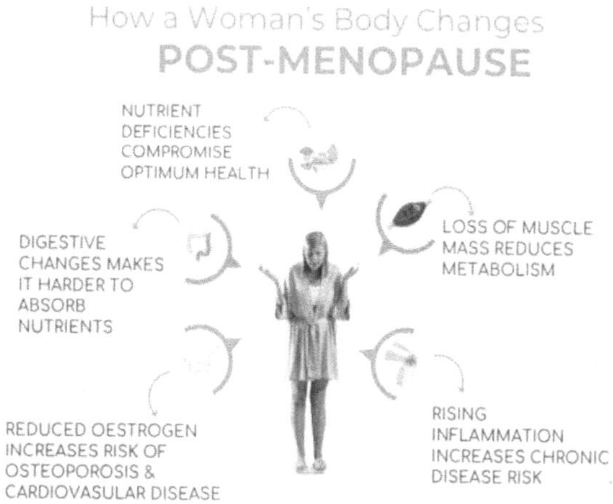

Pic 81: https://www.newdawnhealth.co.uk/

Heart health also requires more attention. Before menopause, estrogen helps protect against heart disease. After menopause, women's risk of heart disease increases. This makes it even more important to maintain healthy blood pressure, cholesterol levels, and weight.

Sexual health may continue to be affected by vaginal dryness and decreased libido. However, many women find that with proper care and communication with their partners, they can maintain satisfying intimate relationships throughout their post-menopausal years.

Common Health Problems during This Life Stage

Hot Flashes and Night Sweats

Hot flashes are one of the most common and bothersome symptoms of menopause. They affect up to 75% of women going through menopause. A hot flash typically starts as a sudden feeling of heat in your chest and face, spreading throughout your body. Your skin may become red and flushed, and you may sweat heavily.

Hot flashes can last anywhere from 30 seconds to 10 minutes, with most lasting about 4 minutes. They can happen once a day or multiple times per hour. When they occur at night, they're called night sweats and can seriously disrupt your sleep.

To manage hot flashes naturally, identify and avoid your triggers. Common triggers include spicy foods, alcohol, caffeine, stress, tight clothing, and hot weather or heated rooms. Keep a diary to track when hot flashes occur and what might have triggered them.

Lifestyle changes that can help include dressing in layers so you can remove clothing when you feel hot, keeping your environment cool with fans or air conditioning when possible, practicing relaxation techniques like deep breathing or meditation, maintaining a healthy weight, and exercising regularly.

When a hot flash starts, try slow, deep breathing, drinking cold water, using a handheld fan, removing layers of clothing, and placing a cold pack on your neck or wrists.

Sleep Problems

Sleep disturbances are very common during perimenopause and menopause. You may have trouble falling asleep, wake up frequently during the night, experience night sweats that wake you up, or wake up very early and be unable to go back to sleep.

Poor sleep can make other menopause symptoms worse, including mood changes, difficulty concentrating, and physical fatigue. It can also affect your immune system and overall health.

To improve your sleep, maintain a regular sleep schedule by going to bed and waking up at the same times every day. Create a cool, comfortable sleeping environment and keep your bedroom dark and quiet. Avoid caffeine, alcohol, and large meals close to bedtime.

Develop a relaxing bedtime routine such as reading, gentle stretching, or taking a warm bath. Limit screen time from phones, computers, or TV before bed. If you can't fall asleep within 20 minutes, get up and do a quiet activity until you feel sleepy.

If night sweats are disrupting your sleep, keep extra nightclothes and towels nearby, use moisture-wicking bedding materials, keep a cold pack or wet cloth by your bed, and consider using a fan in your bedroom.

Mood Changes and Depression

Hormonal fluctuations during perimenopause and menopause can significantly affect your mood and emotional well-being. You may experience irritability, anxiety, sadness, or mood swings that seem to come from nowhere.

Some women develop depression during this time, especially if they have a history of depression or are dealing with other major life stresses. It's important to recognize that these mood changes are real and often related to hormonal changes, not personal weakness or failure.

Signs that you may need additional support include persistent sadness or hopelessness that lasts for weeks, loss of interest in activities you used to enjoy, significant changes in appetite or weight, difficulty making decisions or concentrating, feelings of worthlessness or excessive guilt, thoughts of death or suicide, or inability to function in your daily life.

To support your mental health naturally, maintain social connections with friends and family, engage in regular physical activity which naturally improves mood, practice stress- reduction techniques like meditation, prayer, or yoga, pursue hobbies and activities that bring you joy, get adequate sleep and nutrition, and limit alcohol consumption.

Don't hesitate to seek professional help if mood changes are severe or interfering with your life. Depression during menopause is treatable, and getting help is a sign of strength, not weakness.

Weight Gain and Body Changes

Many women notice weight gain during perimenopause and menopause, particularly around the waist and abdomen. This happens due to hormonal changes that affect how your body stores fat, a slowing metabolism as you age, and often reduced physical activity.

The average woman gains about 5 pounds during menopause, but some women gain much more. This weight gain isn't just cosmetic - extra weight, especially around the waist, increases your risk of diabetes, heart disease, and other health problems.

To manage weight during menopause, focus on eating nutrient-dense foods including plenty of vegetables, fruits, whole grains, and lean proteins. Control portion sizes and avoid eating large meals late in the evening. Limit processed foods, sugary drinks, and excessive amounts of refined carbohydrates.

Stay physically active with both cardiovascular exercise and strength training. As you age, maintaining muscle mass becomes increasingly important for keeping your metabolism active. Even simple activities like walking, gardening, or household chores can help.

Remember that some body changes are normal and natural. Your body shape may change even if your weight stays the same. Focus on being healthy and strong rather than trying to maintain the exact same body you had in your 20s or 30s.

Bone Health and Osteoporosis

After menopause, the loss of estrogen accelerates bone loss, making osteoporosis a significant concern. Osteoporosis makes bones weak and brittle, increasing the risk of fractures from even minor falls or bumps.

The good news is that there are many things you can do to protect your bone health. Weight-bearing exercises like walking, dancing, or stair climbing help maintain bone density. Resistance exercises using weights or resistance bands also strengthen bones.

Nutrition plays a crucial role in bone health. Ensure adequate calcium intake through dairy products, green leafy vegetables, sardines, or calcium supplements if recommended by a doctor. Vitamin D is equally important as it helps your body absorb calcium. You can get vitamin D from sunlight, certain foods, or supplements.

Lifestyle factors that protect bones include not smoking, limiting alcohol consumption, preventing falls by keeping your home well-lit and removing tripping hazards, and maintaining good posture and balance.

Risk factors for osteoporosis include being thin or small-framed, having a family history of osteoporosis, not getting enough calcium or vitamin D, lack of physical activity, smoking, excessive alcohol consumption, and certain medications.

Heart Disease Risk

Before menopause, estrogen helps protect women against heart disease. After menopause, women's risk of heart disease increases significantly and eventually equals that of men. This makes heart health a crucial focus during and after menopause.

To protect your heart health, maintain a healthy blood pressure by limiting salt intake, managing stress, maintaining a healthy weight, and exercising regularly. Monitor your cholesterol levels and work with healthcare providers to keep them in a healthy range.

Don't smoke, and if you do smoke, quit. Smoking dramatically increases your risk of heart disease, especially after menopause. Limit alcohol consumption to moderate amounts, if any.

Manage diabetes if you have it, as diabetes significantly increases heart disease risk. Keep blood sugar levels as close to normal as possible through diet, exercise, and medication if prescribed.

Recognize the signs of heart problems, which can be different in women than in men. While chest pain is common, women may experience shortness of breath, nausea, back pain, jaw pain, or extreme fatigue without chest pain.

Sexual Health Changes

Menopause brings changes to sexual health that many women find challenging to discuss. Lower estrogen levels can cause vaginal dryness, thinning of vaginal tissues, and reduced elasticity. These changes can make sexual intercourse uncomfortable or painful.

Decreased libido or interest in sex is also common during and after menopause. This can be due to hormonal changes, physical discomfort, body image concerns, relationship issues, or other life stresses.

These changes don't mean the end of your sexual life. There are many ways to maintain intimacy and sexual satisfaction. Use water-based lubricants or moisturizers to address vaginal dryness. Take time for adequate foreplay and communicate openly with your partner about what feels comfortable.

Regular sexual activity, whether with a partner or alone, can help maintain vaginal health by increasing blood flow to the area. Kegel exercises, which strengthen the pelvic floor muscles, can also improve sexual function and bladder control.

Don't suffer in silence with sexual health problems. Healthcare providers can offer treatments ranging from topical estrogen creams to other medications that can help restore comfort and function.

Managing Symptoms Naturally

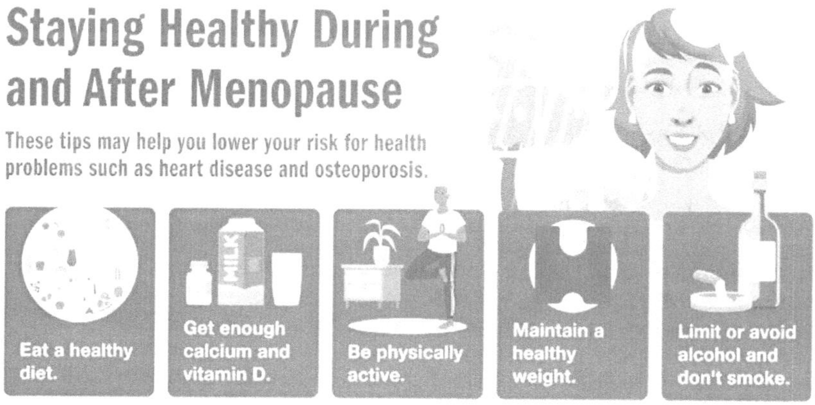

Pic 82: https://www.nia.nih.gov/

Dietary Approaches

What you eat can significantly impact how you experience menopause symptoms. A healthy, balanced diet provides your body with the nutrients it needs during this transition and can help minimize uncomfortable symptoms.

Focus on eating plenty of fruits and vegetables, which provide antioxidants and nutrients that support overall health. Aim for a variety of colors to ensure you're getting different vitamins and minerals. Include whole grains, which provide steady energy and help maintain stable blood sugar levels.

Some foods may help with specific menopausal symptoms. Soy products like tofu, soy milk, and edamame contain natural plant compounds called phytoestrogens that may help reduce hot flashes in some women. Flaxseeds are another source of phytoestrogens and also provide healthy omega-3 fats.

Foods rich in calcium and vitamin D support bone health. Good sources include dairy products, leafy green vegetables, sardines with bones, and fortified foods. If you can't get enough from food, supplements may be necessary.

Stay hydrated by drinking plenty of water throughout the day. Dehydration can worsen hot flashes and contribute to other uncomfortable symptoms.

Limit or avoid foods that may trigger hot flashes or worsen symptoms. These often include spicy foods, caffeine, alcohol, and very hot foods or drinks. Keep a food diary to identify your personal triggers.

Herbal Remedies and Natural Supplements

Many women find relief from menopause symptoms using herbal remedies and natural supplements. While scientific evidence varies for different remedies, many women report benefits from certain natural approaches.

Black cohosh is one of the most studied herbs for menopause symptoms, particularly hot flashes. Some women find it helpful, though results vary. Red clover is another herb that contains phytoestrogens and may help some women with hot flashes.

Evening primrose oil is sometimes used for breast tenderness and mood symptoms. Valerian root may help with sleep problems and anxiety. Ginseng is sometimes recommended for mood and energy, though evidence is mixed.

It's important to remember that "natural" doesn't always mean safe. Herbs can interact with medications and may not be appropriate for everyone. Always talk to a healthcare provider before starting any herbal remedies, especially if you take other medications or have health conditions.

Some supplements that may be helpful include calcium and vitamin D for bone health, omega-3 fatty acids for heart health and mood, magnesium for sleep and muscle relaxation, and B- complex vitamins for energy and mood support.

Exercise and Physical Activity

Regular exercise is one of the most effective ways to manage menopause symptoms and protect your long-term health. Exercise can reduce hot flashes, improve sleep, boost mood, help with weight management, and protect against osteoporosis and heart disease.

Cardiovascular exercise like walking, swimming, dancing, or cycling helps maintain heart health and can reduce hot flashes. Aim for at least 30 minutes of moderate activity most days of the week. If you're not used to exercise, start slowly and gradually increase your activity level.

Strength training becomes especially important during and after menopause. Resistance exercises help maintain muscle mass, which naturally decreases with age, and help protect bone density. You don't need expensive equipment - bodyweight exercises, resistance bands, or simple weights can be very effective.

Flexibility and balance exercises like yoga, tai chi, or simple stretching help maintain mobility and reduce the risk of falls. These activities can also help with stress management and improve sleep quality.

Find activities you enjoy so you're more likely to stick with them. Exercise doesn't have to mean going to a gym - gardening, dancing, playing with grandchildren, or household chores all count as physical activity.

Listen to your body and adjust your activities as needed. Some days you may have more energy than others, and that's normal. The key is to stay consistently active rather than doing intense exercise occasionally.

Stress Management

Stress can worsen many menopause symptoms, including hot flashes, sleep problems, and mood changes. Learning to manage stress effectively can significantly improve your quality of life during this transition.

Deep breathing exercises are simple but effective for managing stress and may even help reduce hot flashes when they occur. Practice breathing slowly and deeply, focusing on your breath rather than your worries.

Meditation, prayer, or quiet reflection can help calm your mind and reduce stress. Even a few minutes of quiet time each day can make a difference. You don't need special training - simply sitting quietly and focusing on peaceful thoughts can be beneficial.

Pic 83: https://www.everydayhealth.com/meditation/guide/

Regular physical activity is one of the best stress relievers. Exercise releases natural mood-boosting chemicals in your brain and provides a healthy outlet for stress and tension.

Maintain social connections with friends and family. Talking about your experiences with trusted people who understand can provide emotional support and reduce feelings of isolation.

Consider learning new relaxation techniques like progressive muscle relaxation, where you systematically tense and then relax different muscle groups, or guided imagery, where you imagine peaceful, calming scenes.

Make time for activities you enjoy, whether that's reading, crafts, music, or hobbies. Having something to look forward to and enjoy can significantly improve your mood and stress levels.

When to Seek Medical Help

Normal vs. Concerning Symptoms

While menopause is a natural process, some symptoms warrant medical attention. It's important to distinguish between normal menopausal changes and signs of other health problems.

Normal menopause symptoms include irregular periods that gradually stop, hot flashes and night sweats, mood changes and irritability, sleep disturbances, vaginal dryness, decreased libido, weight gain, and joint aches and stiffness.

You should seek medical attention if you experience very heavy bleeding that soaks through a pad or tampon every hour for several hours, bleeding that lasts more than seven days, bleeding that occurs more frequently than every 21 days, or any bleeding after you've been without periods for 12 months.

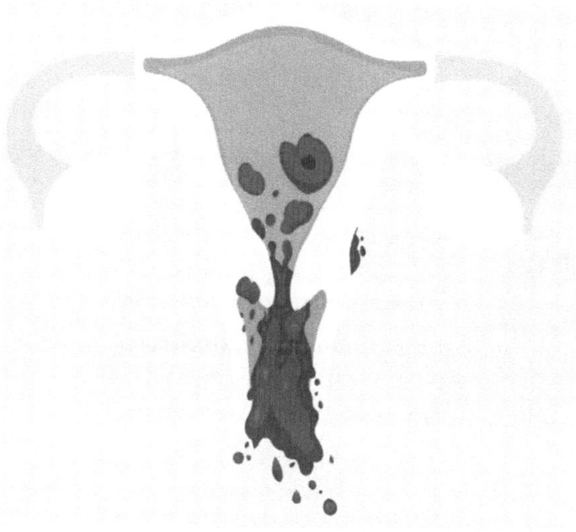

Pic 84: https://www.narayanahealth.org/

Other concerning symptoms include severe depression or thoughts of self-harm, hot flashes that are so severe they interfere with your daily life and don't improve with lifestyle changes, persistent insomnia that doesn't improve with good sleep habits, severe joint pain or stiffness that limits your movement, or any new or unusual symptoms that worry you.

Available Treatments

If lifestyle changes aren't enough to manage your symptoms, there are medical treatments available. Hormone replacement therapy (HRT) involves taking estrogen alone or estrogen combined with progestin to replace the hormones your ovaries no longer produce.

HRT can be very effective for hot flashes, night sweats, vaginal dryness, and may help protect against bone loss. However, it also has risks, including increased risk of blood clots, stroke, and certain types of cancer. The decision about whether HRT is right for you should be made with a healthcare provider based on your individual health history and symptoms.

Non-hormonal medications can also help with specific symptoms. Certain antidepressants can reduce hot flashes even in women who aren't depressed. Blood pressure medications called clonidine can also help with hot flashes. For severe mood symptoms, counselling or antidepressant medications may be helpful.

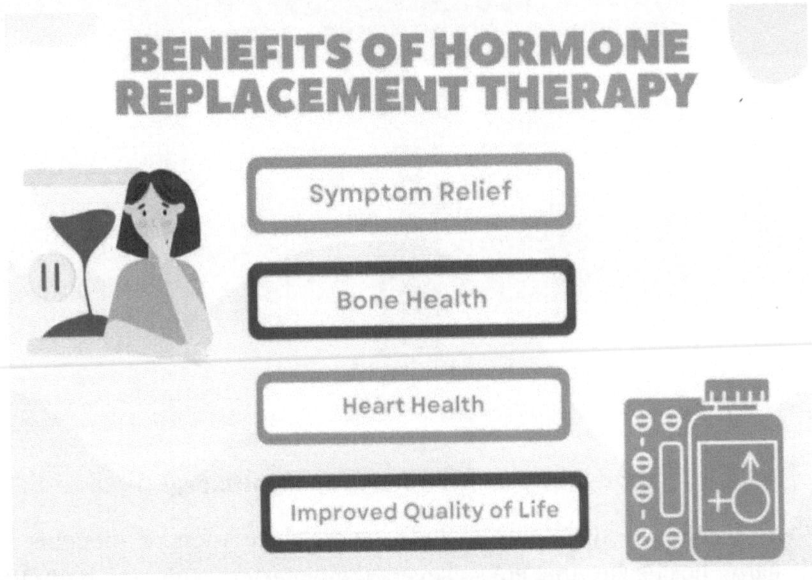

Pic 85: https://www.gardenobgyn.com/

For vaginal dryness and discomfort, low-dose vaginal estrogen creams, tablets, or rings can be effective and have fewer risks than systemic hormone therapy. Over-the-counter lubricants and moisturizers can also provide relief.

Regular Health Screenings

During and after menopause, regular health screenings become even more important. Your risk for several health conditions increases after menopause, making early detection and prevention crucial.

Bone density testing (DEXA scan) should be done around the time of menopause and repeated as recommended to monitor bone health and detect osteoporosis early. Mammograms for breast cancer screening should continue annually or as recommended by your doctor.

Pap smears and pelvic exams should continue as recommended to screen for cervical and other gynecological cancers. Even after menopause, these screenings remain important.

Heart disease screening including blood pressure monitoring, cholesterol testing, and diabetes screening becomes increasingly important after menopause. Your doctor may recommend more frequent monitoring based on your individual risk factors.

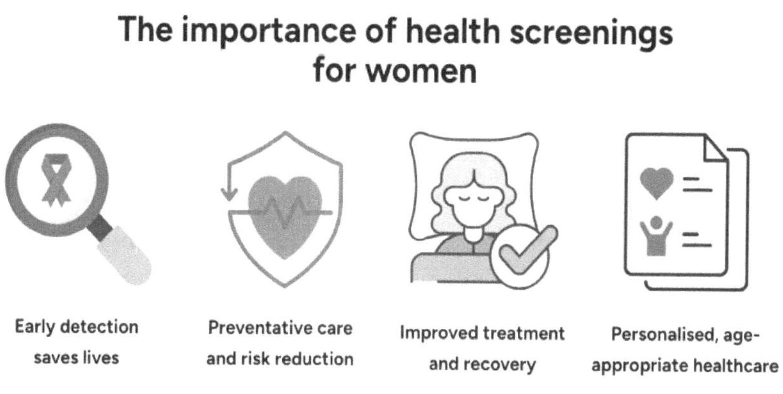

Pic 86: https://www.thomsonmedical.com/

Colon cancer screening typically begins at age 50 but may be recommended earlier based on family history or other risk factors. Skin cancer screening should also be part of your regular health care.

Cultural Myths and Facts about Menopause

Common Misconceptions

Many cultures have myths and misconceptions about menopause that can cause unnecessary fear or shame. Understanding the facts can help you approach this life stage with confidence and accurate information.

One common myth is that menopause means the end of a woman's usefulness or attractiveness. The truth is that menopause is simply the end of fertility, not the end of a woman's value, health, or ability to contribute to her family and community. Many women find their post-menopausal years to be among the most fulfilling of their lives.

Another myth is that all women become depressed or "crazy" during menopause. While mood changes are common, most women navigate menopause without developing serious mental health problems. The majority of women find that emotional symptoms improve after the transition is complete.

Some people believe that menopause happens suddenly overnight. In reality, menopause is a gradual process that typically takes several years. Understanding this can help you prepare for and manage the changes as they occur.

There's also a myth that nothing can be done about menopause symptoms, and women just have to suffer through them. The truth is that there are many effective treatments available, from lifestyle changes to medical interventions, that can significantly improve quality of life during this transition.

Positive Aspects of Menopause

While much attention is given to the challenges of menopause, there are also positive aspects that deserve recognition. Many women report feeling a sense of freedom after menopause because they no longer have to worry about pregnancy or dealing with monthly periods.

Some women experience increased energy and focus once their hormones stabilize after the menopausal transition. Without the monthly fluctuations of hormones, many women find their moods become more stable and predictable.

This life stage often coincides with increased independence and self-confidence. Children may be grown and more independent, allowing women to focus more on their own interests and goals. Many women find this a time of personal growth and new opportunities.

Pic 87: https://www.istockphoto.com/

Sexual intimacy can actually improve for some women after menopause, particularly if they had concerns about pregnancy previously. While physical changes may require some adjustments, many couples find ways to maintain or even improve their intimate relationship.

Nutrition and Lifestyle in Later Years

Nutritional Needs after Menopause

Your nutritional needs change during and after menopause. With a slower metabolism and hormonal changes, it becomes even more important to focus on nutrient-dense foods that provide the vitamins and minerals your body needs without excess calories.

Calcium requirements increase to help protect bone health. Post-menopausal women need about 1,200 mg of calcium daily, which can be challenging to get from food alone. Good sources include dairy products, leafy green vegetables, sardines with bones, and calcium-fortified foods.

Vitamin D becomes increasingly important as you age because it helps your body absorb calcium and supports bone health. Your skin becomes less efficient at producing vitamin D from sunlight as you age, so supplements may be necessary.

Protein needs may actually increase slightly after menopause to help maintain muscle mass. Include protein-rich foods at each meal, such as beans, lentils, eggs, dairy products, fish, or meat if your family eats it.

Iron needs decrease after menopause because you're no longer losing iron through menstrual bleeding. However, iron-rich foods are still important for overall health and energy.

Limit sodium to help control blood pressure and reduce your risk of heart disease. Many processed and packaged foods are high in sodium, so focus on fresh, whole foods when possible.

Stay hydrated by drinking plenty of water throughout the day. As you age, your sense of thirst may decrease, making it easy to become dehydrated without realizing it.

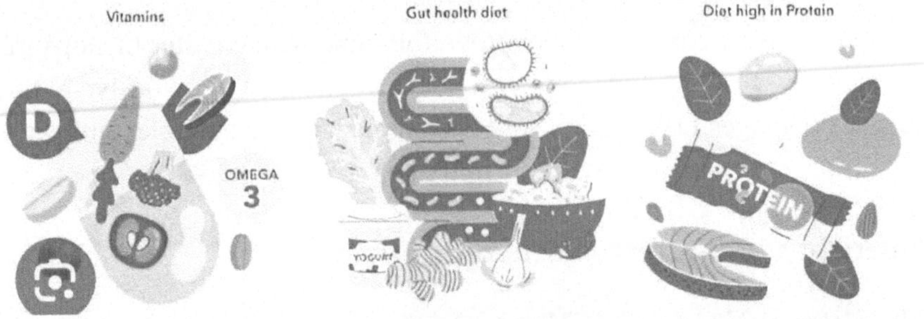

Pic 88: https://www.shutterstock.com/image- vector/nutritional-essentials-set-key-vitamins-health- 2441719705

Maintaining Physical Activity

Staying physically active becomes even more important as you age. Regular exercise helps maintain bone density, muscle mass, balance, and cardiovascular health. It also supports mental health and can help prevent many age-related health problems.

If you haven't been active, it's never too late to start. Begin slowly with gentle activities like walking, and gradually increase your activity level as your fitness improves. Even small amounts of activity are beneficial.

Include different types of exercise for maximum benefit. Cardiovascular activities like walking, swimming, or dancing help maintain heart health and stamina. Strength training helps preserve muscle mass and bone density. Flexibility exercises help maintain range of motion and prevent stiffness.

Balance exercises become increasingly important to prevent falls, which can be serious as you age. Simple exercises like standing on one foot, walking heel-to-toe, or gentle yoga poses can help improve balance.

Make physical activity a social activity when possible. Walk with friends, join a dance class, or participate in community activities. The social aspect can make exercise more enjoyable and help you stick with it.

Listen to your body and adjust activities based on how you feel. Some days you may need gentler activities, and that's perfectly normal. The goal is consistent movement rather than intense exercise.

Sleep and Rest

Quality sleep remains important throughout your life but can become more challenging as you age. Hormonal changes, health conditions, medications, and life stresses can all affect sleep quality.

Maintain good sleep habits by going to bed and waking up at consistent times, keeping your bedroom cool, dark, and quiet, avoiding caffeine and alcohol close to bedtime, and creating a relaxing bedtime routine.

If you're having trouble sleeping, avoid napping during the day, as this can interfere with nighttime sleep. If you must nap, keep it short (20-30 minutes) and early in the afternoon.

Physical discomfort from conditions like arthritis or hot flashes can interfere with sleep. Address these issues with appropriate treatments to improve your sleep quality.

Some medications can affect sleep, so discuss any sleep problems with your healthcare provider. They may be able to adjust medications or timing to improve your sleep.

If sleep problems persist despite good sleep habits, don't hesitate to seek help. Poor sleep affects your physical health, mental health, and quality of life, so it's worth addressing.

Building Support Networks

Family Relationships

Menopause can affect family relationships in various ways. Some women find that hormonal changes make them more irritable or emotionally sensitive, which can strain relationships with spouses and children. Open communication about what you're experiencing can help family members understand and support you.

Your relationship with your spouse or partner may require some adjustments during this time. Physical changes like vaginal dryness can affect intimacy, while mood changes and sleep disruptions can affect daily interactions. Patience, understanding, and open communication from both partners are essential.

If you have adult children, this can be a time to develop new, more mature relationships with them. As they become independent adults, you may find opportunities to connect in different ways and perhaps develop friendships as well as parent-child relationships.

Your relationship with your own aging parents may also be changing during this time. You may find yourself in a caregiving role while simultaneously dealing with your own health changes. Don't hesitate to ask for help and support from siblings or other family members.

Chapter - 5
Staying Strong in Later Years

Priya at 65 - New Challenges, Continued Strength

Priya was now 65 years old, and her life had changed in ways she never expected. Her daughter was married with children of her own, and Priya had become a beloved grandmother to two beautiful grandchildren. Her husband Raj had retired from the bank, and they were learning to spend more time together after decades of busy working lives.

But with age came new health challenges. Priya noticed that climbing stairs made her knees ache, her vision wasn't as sharp as it used to be, and she sometimes felt dizzy when she stood up quickly. Her mother, now 85, needed more help with daily tasks, and Priya found herself juggling her own health needs with caring for her aging parent.

One morning, during a routine health check-up, the doctor told Priya that her blood sugar levels were higher than normal. "You're developing diabetes," the doctor explained gently. "This is common as we age, but with proper care, you can manage it well and continue to live a healthy life."

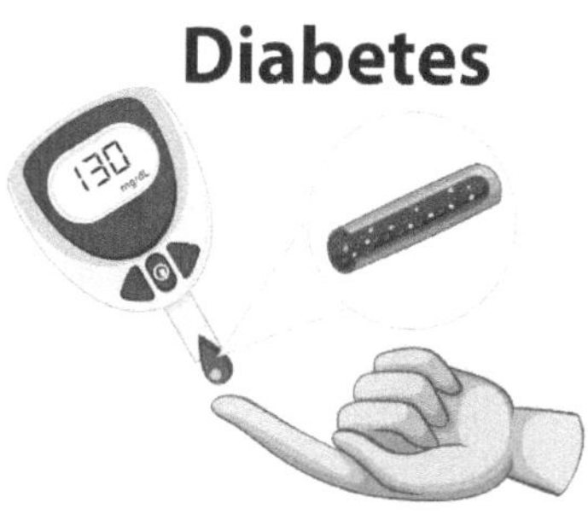

Pic 89: https://www.freepik.com/vectors

Priya felt scared and overwhelmed. How could she take care of her mother, help with her grandchildren, manage her own health problems, and still maintain her independence? Through conversations with her doctor, other women her age, and her own determination, she learned that aging with dignity and health was not only possible but could be rewarding.

Common Health Challenges After 60

As women age beyond 60, their bodies face new challenges that require attention and care. Understanding these changes helps you prepare for them and manage them effectively. Most age-related health problems can be controlled or slowed down with proper care, allowing you to maintain your quality of life.

Diabetes - Managing Blood Sugar

Diabetes becomes increasingly common as women age, affecting nearly one in four women over 60. Type 2 diabetes develops when your body cannot use insulin properly to control blood sugar levels. This condition can develop gradually over years, often without obvious symptoms in the early stages.

Understanding the symptoms is crucial for early detection. You may feel extremely thirsty and need to urinate frequently, especially at night. Unexplained weight loss despite eating normally, constant fatigue and weakness, blurred vision that comes and goes, cuts or bruises that heal slowly, frequent infections, particularly urinary tract infections or yeast infections, and tingling or numbness in your hands or feet can all be signs of diabetes.

Several factors increase your risk of developing diabetes as you age. Being overweight, especially carrying extra weight around your waist, significantly increases risk. A family history of diabetes, previous gestational diabetes during pregnancy, high blood pressure, and a sedentary lifestyle all contribute to increased risk. Certain ethnic groups also have higher rates of diabetes.

The good news is that diabetes can be prevented and managed effectively. Maintaining a healthy weight through proper diet and regular exercise is the most important prevention strategy. Eat plenty of vegetables, whole grains, and lean proteins while limiting processed foods, sugary drinks, and refined carbohydrates. Regular physical activity, even just walking for 30 minutes daily, can significantly reduce your risk.

If you're diagnosed with diabetes, don't panic. With proper management, you can live a full, healthy life. Monitor your blood sugar levels as directed by your healthcare provider. Take prescribed medications exactly as directed, even when you feel fine. Keep regular appointments with your healthcare team to monitor your condition and adjust treatment as needed.

Pay special attention to foot care because diabetes can reduce blood flow and sensation in your feet. Check your feet daily for cuts, blisters, or changes in color. Wear well-fitting shoes and never go barefoot. Keep your feet clean and dry, and see a healthcare provider immediately if you notice any problems.

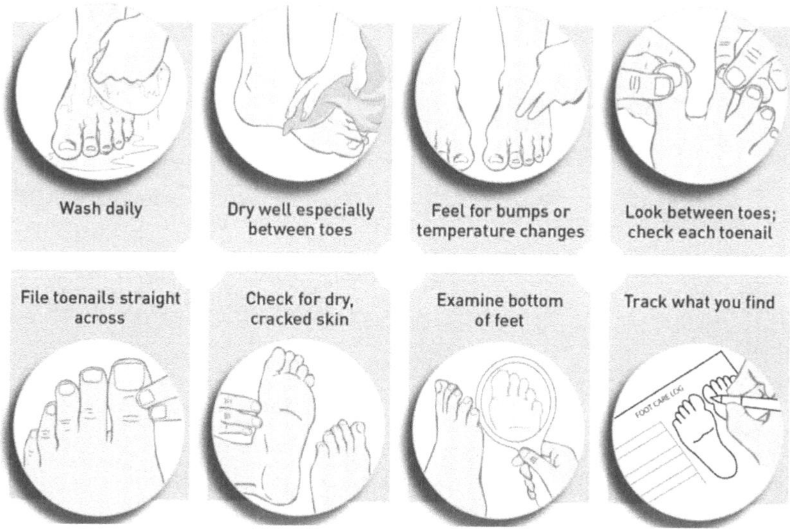

Pic 90: https://www.crh.org/

Watch for signs of complications that require immediate medical attention. These include extremely high or low blood sugar symptoms such as confusion, dizziness, rapid heartbeat, or loss of consciousness. Severe dehydration with dry mouth, extreme thirst, and little or no urination also requires emergency care. Any signs of serious infection, particularly if you have a fever, should be evaluated promptly.

Arthritis - Protecting Your Joints

Arthritis affects millions of women, particularly as they age. The most common type is osteoarthritis, which occurs when the cartilage that cushions your joints wears down over time. This can cause pain, stiffness, and reduced mobility, but there are many ways to manage symptoms and maintain an active life.

Joint pain and stiffness, particularly in the morning or after periods of inactivity, are the most common symptoms. You may notice that certain joints, such as your knees, hips, fingers, or spine, are more affected than others. The pain may be worse in cold or damp weather, and you might hear crackling sounds when you move certain joints.

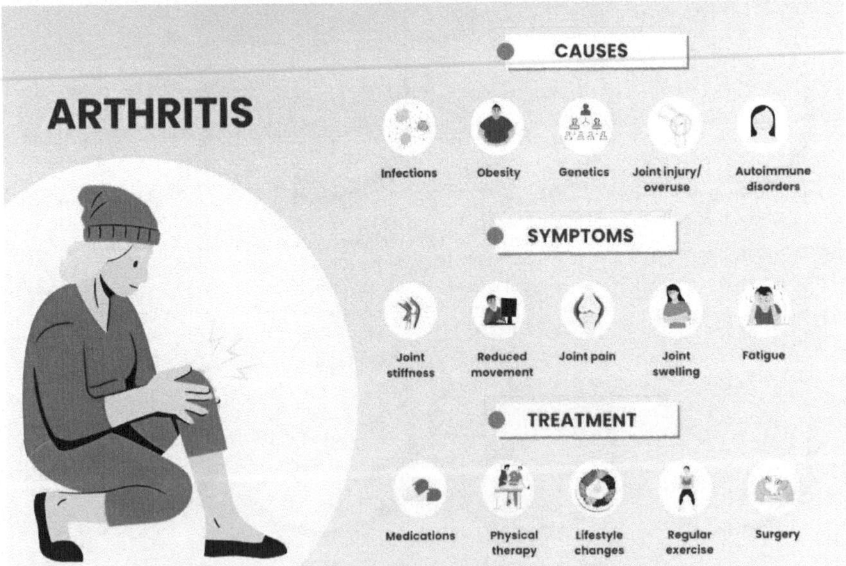

Pic 91: https://www.manipalhospitals.com/

While you can't completely prevent arthritis, you can reduce your risk and slow its progression. Maintaining a healthy weight reduces stress on weight-bearing joints like your knees and hips. Regular exercise keeps joints flexible and strengthens the muscles that support them. Protect your joints from injury by using proper body mechanics when lifting or carrying objects.

Managing arthritis pain requires a combination of approaches. Gentle exercise is one of the most effective treatments. Swimming, walking, or simple stretching exercises can help maintain flexibility and reduce stiffness. Apply heat to stiff joints in the morning and cold to painful joints after activity.

Over-the-counter pain medications can provide relief, but use them carefully and talk to your healthcare provider about the best options for you. Some people find relief from natural remedies like turmeric or ginger, but always discuss these with your doctor first, especially if you take other medications.

Physical therapy can teach you exercises and techniques to manage pain and maintain mobility. Occupational therapy can help you learn new ways to perform daily tasks that put less stress on your joints.

Know when arthritis pain requires medical attention. See your healthcare provider if joint pain is severe and doesn't improve with rest and home treatments, if you have signs of infection such as fever, redness, or warmth around a joint, if pain interferes significantly with your daily activities or sleep, or if you experience sudden, severe joint pain.

High Blood Pressure - The Silent Threat

High blood pressure, also called hypertension, is often called the "silent killer" because it usually has no symptoms but can cause serious damage to your heart, brain, kidneys, and other organs. Nearly two-thirds of women over 60 have high blood pressure, making it one of the most common health challenges of aging.

Most people with high blood pressure feel perfectly normal, which is why regular monitoring is so important. Occasionally, very high blood pressure may cause headaches, dizziness, nosebleeds, or shortness of breath, but you cannot rely on symptoms to know if your blood pressure is elevated.

Understanding blood pressure numbers helps you take control of your health. Blood pressure is measured with two numbers. The top number (systolic) measures pressure when your heart beats, and the bottom number (diastolic) measures pressure when your heart rests between beats. Normal blood pressure is less than 120/80. High blood pressure is 130/80 or higher.

Many factors contribute to high blood pressure as you age. Your blood vessels become less flexible over time, making it harder for blood to flow smoothly. Excess weight, too much salt in your diet, lack of physical activity, chronic stress, and certain medical conditions can all raise blood pressure.

The good news is that lifestyle changes can significantly lower blood pressure. Reduce sodium in your diet by limiting processed foods, restaurant meals, and adding salt to food. Eat plenty of fruits, vegetables, and whole grains. The DASH diet (Dietary Approaches to Stop Hypertension) has been proven effective for lowering blood pressure.

Stay physically active with at least 30 minutes of moderate exercise most days of the week. Walking, swimming, dancing, or gardening all count as physical activity. Maintain a healthy weight, as even small weight losses can make a difference in blood pressure.

Manage stress through relaxation techniques, deep breathing, meditation, or activities you enjoy. Limit alcohol consumption and don't smoke, as both can raise blood pressure.

If lifestyle changes aren't enough, medications can effectively control blood pressure. Many different types of blood pressure medications are available, and your healthcare provider can find the right combination for you. Take medications exactly as prescribed, even when you feel fine. Don't stop taking blood pressure medications without consulting your healthcare provider.

Monitor your blood pressure regularly at home if possible, or have it checked regularly at a pharmacy or healthcare facility. Keep track of your readings and share them with your healthcare provider.

High blood pressure is particularly dangerous because it increases your risk of heart attack, stroke, kidney disease, and other serious complications. But with proper management, you can significantly reduce these risks and maintain good health.

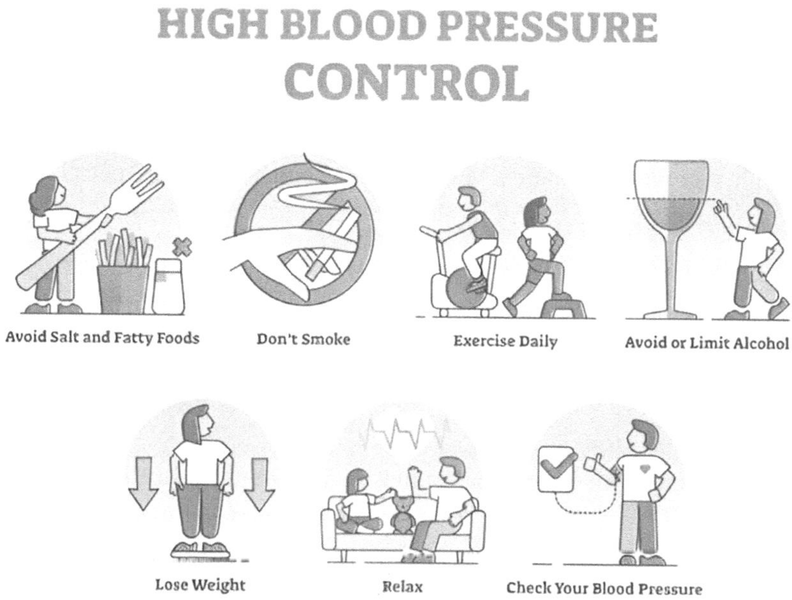

Pic 92: https://www.shutterstock.com/

Vision and Hearing Changes

Changes in vision and hearing are common as we age, but they don't have to drastically impact your quality of life. Understanding what's normal and what requires medical attention can help you maintain your independence and safety.

Vision changes often develop gradually. You may find that you need more light for reading or close work. Small print becomes harder to see, and you might need to hold things farther away to focus on them. Colors may seem less vibrant, and you may have more difficulty seeing in low light or adjusting to changes in lighting.

Some vision changes are more serious and require prompt medical attention. These include sudden vision loss, flashing lights or new floaters in your vision, severe eye pain, halos around lights, or a curtain-like shadow across your field of vision.

Common age-related vision problems include presbyopia, which makes it hard to focus on close objects and is easily corrected with reading glasses. Cataracts cause cloudy vision and can be treated with surgery. Glaucoma can cause vision loss but can be managed if detected early through regular eye exams. Macular degeneration affects central vision but peripheral vision usually remains intact.

Protect your vision by having regular eye exams, at least every two years after age 60. Wear sunglasses to protect against UV damage. Eat foods rich in vitamins A, C, and E, such as leafy green vegetables, carrots, and citrus fruits. Don't smoke, as smoking significantly increases the risk of eye diseases.

Hearing changes also develop gradually. You may find it harder to hear in noisy environments or to distinguish between similar sounds. You might need to turn up the TV or radio, or ask people to repeat themselves more often.

Signs of hearing loss that should be evaluated include difficulty following conversations, especially in groups or noisy places, frequently asking people to repeat themselves, turning up the volume on TV or radio louder than others prefer, feeling like people are mumbling, or avoiding social situations because it's hard to hear.

Pic 93: https://www.shutterstock.com/

Protect your hearing by avoiding loud noises when possible, wearing ear protection in loud environments, and cleaning your ears gently. Never insert objects into your ears. If you notice hearing changes, see a healthcare provider for evaluation. Hearing aids can significantly improve quality of life for many people with hearing loss.

Memory and Cognitive Health

Some changes in memory and thinking are normal as we age, but significant changes that interfere with daily life are not normal and should be evaluated by a healthcare provider.

Normal age-related changes might include occasionally forgetting names or appointments but remembering them later, sometimes having trouble finding the right word, occasionally misplacing items, or taking longer to learn new information.

More concerning changes include getting lost in familiar places, forgetting how to do familiar tasks, repeating questions or stories in the same conversation, having trouble following directions or recipes, becoming confused about time, people, or places, or experiencing significant personality changes.

Pic 94: https://www.shutterstock.com/

You can support your brain health through regular physical exercise, which increases blood flow to the brain and may help maintain cognitive function. Stay mentally active by reading, doing puzzles, learning new skills, or engaging in stimulating conversations. Maintain social connections, as isolation can contribute to cognitive decline.

Eat a healthy diet rich in fruits, vegetables, whole grains, and omega-3 fatty acids found in fish. Get adequate sleep, as poor sleep can affect memory and cognitive function. Manage chronic conditions like diabetes and high blood pressure, as these can affect brain health.

Limit alcohol consumption and don't smoke, as both can harm brain function. Manage stress through relaxation techniques, as chronic stress can affect memory and cognitive function.

The Challenges of Caregiving

Becoming a Caregiver

Many women in their 60s and beyond become caregivers, often while also managing their own health problems. Caregiving usually begins with small tasks such as running errands or taking someone to appointments, but over time it can grow into daily personal care or even round-the-clock support. Some women find themselves caring for more than one person at the same time, such as aging parents, spouses, or grandchildren, which makes the responsibility even heavier.

Health Impacts of Caregiving

Caregiving is rewarding, but it can take a serious toll on health. The physical strain, poor sleep, and constant stress can weaken the body, while skipping your own medical appointments or medicines only makes things worse. Mentally and emotionally, caregivers often feel depressed, anxious, guilty, or isolated. Financial pressure can add another layer of stress, especially if you have to cut back on work or spend extra money on care.

Pic 95: https://www.shutterstock.com/

Caring for Yourself While Caring for Others

Taking care of yourself while you care for others is not selfish—it is necessary. Set realistic expectations and remember that your role is to provide safe and adequate care, not perfection. Make your health a priority by keeping medical appointments, taking your medicines on time, eating nutritious meals, resting properly, and staying as active as possible. Talking about your feelings with friends, family, or support groups helps lighten the emotional load, and practicing relaxation techniques such as deep breathing or prayer can calm the mind. It is also important to ask for and accept help. Share responsibilities with family members or reach out to community support programs instead of trying to do everything alone. Learning safe ways to lift, move, or assist your loved one can also prevent injuries for both of you.

Finding Support and Resources

Support can come from many directions. Family members may share tasks, contribute financially, or simply provide encouragement. Community and religious organizations often offer meal services, day care, or volunteer help. Government programs sometimes provide financial aid or home-based services. Professionals such as nurses, social workers, or counselors can guide you through medical needs, paperwork, or emotional struggles.

When Professional Care Is Needed

Despite your best efforts, there may come a time when care at home is no longer safe. If your loved one needs help with nearly all daily activities, shows severe memory problems, requires complex medical care, or if your own health begins to fail, it may be time to consider professional care. Options include home health aides, adult day programs, assisted living facilities, or nursing homes. Choosing professional care is not a failure—it is a responsible decision that ensures safety and well-being for everyone.

Maintaining Independence and Quality of Life

Even while caregiving, it is important to maintain your own independence and quality of life as you age. Staying physically active through walking, light household work, or simple exercises helps keep muscles strong and balance steady. Keeping the mind active by reading, learning new skills, playing games, or staying organized supports memory and sharpness. A safe living environment also matters: removing tripping hazards, improving lighting, and adding grab bars can prevent accidents. Finally, staying socially connected— through family visits, community activities, phone calls, or even video chats—protects both mental and emotional health.

Managing Chronic Conditions

Many women over 60 have one or more chronic health conditions such as diabetes, arthritis, or high blood pressure. Successfully managing these conditions is key to maintaining independence and quality of life.

Work closely with your healthcare team to develop management plans for your conditions. This might include taking medications as prescribed, following dietary recommendations, monitoring symptoms or vital signs, and attending regular check-ups.

Learn as much as you can about your health conditions.

Understanding your conditions helps you make informed decisions about your care and recognize when something needs attention.

Pic 96: https://www.dreamstime.com/

Keep organized records of your health information including lists of medications, allergies, healthcare providers, and important medical history. This information is crucial in emergencies and when seeing new healthcare providers.

Don't ignore new symptoms or changes in existing conditions. Early attention to problems often prevents them from becoming more serious.

Consider how your health conditions affect your daily activities and make adaptations as needed. This might involve using assistive devices, modifying your home environment, or changing how you do certain tasks.

Financial Security

Financial security is an important part of independence and quality of life in later years. Since healthcare costs rise with age, it is essential to plan ahead. Know what your insurance covers and budget for expenses that may not be included. Consider options for long-term care, as these services can be costly and are often not fully covered by insurance or government programs.

Be cautious about financial scams, which often target older adults. Never share personal financial details or make quick decisions under pressure. When unsure, consult trusted family members or professionals before making big financial choices.

Keep important financial and legal documents well-organized and let trusted family members know where they are in case of emergency.

Financial independence

Pic 97: https://www.alamy.com/

Your Life Still Has Great Value and Purpose

As Priya learned to take care of her diabetes, help her aging mother, and accept help from others when she needed it, she discovered something important. Getting older didn't mean her life was less valuable or meaningful. In fact, she found new ways to feel useful and happy.

Priya realized that her years of experience had made her wise. She could help her daughter navigate the challenges of raising children. She could comfort friends who were going through difficult times. She could share the lessons she had learned from her own struggles and successes.

When her young granddaughter was afraid of starting school, Priya told her stories of her own fears and how she overcame them. When her neighbor was diagnosed with diabetes, Priya was able to share practical tips about managing the condition. These moments of helping others gave Priya a deep sense of purpose and joy.

You Are Stronger Than You Know

Every woman who reaches her later years has survived many challenges. You have lived through difficulties, celebrated joys, and learned valuable lessons. This experience has made you stronger and wiser than you might realize.

Think about all the things you have accomplished in your life. You may have raised children, cared for family members, worked to support your household, or contributed to your community in countless ways. These accomplishments matter, and they have prepared you to face the challenges of aging with strength and wisdom.

You have survived hardships before, and this experience helps you cope with current problems. You know that difficult times eventually pass. You know that you are capable of adapting to change. You know that there is usually a way to solve problems, even when they seem overwhelming at first.

Pic 98: https://www.istockphoto.com/

Your body may be changing, but your inner strength remains. The courage that helped you through earlier challenges is still within you. The love you have for your family and friends still gives your life meaning. The wisdom you have gained over the years is a precious gift that you can share with others.

Final Words of Encouragement

You have lived a full life with its share of joys and sorrows, challenges and victories. You have loved and been loved. You have learned and grown. You have made a difference in the lives of others, even in ways you might not realize.

The challenges of aging are real, but they don't define you. You are more than your health problems, more than your limitations, more than your fears about the future. You are a woman with a lifetime of experience, wisdom, and love to share.

Take care of your health not as a burden but as a gift you give to yourself and everyone who cares about you. Seek help when you need it not as a defeat but as a wise decision that allows you to continue living well.

Face each day with hope, knowing that you have the strength to handle whatever comes. Find joy in small moments and deep satisfaction in the love you give and receive.

You matter. Your life has value. Your wisdom is needed. Your love makes a difference. You are a remarkable woman who deserves to live her later years with dignity, health, and happiness.

Remember that growing older is not about losing what you once had - it's about appreciating what you have now and making the most of each day you're given. You have the strength, wisdom, and love to make your remaining years meaningful and beautiful. Your journey continues, and it can still be filled with purpose, joy, and love. Trust in yourself, accept the support of others, and know that your best days may still be ahead of you.